BTK –

BIND,

TORTURE, KILL

The Horrifying True Crime Story of Serial Killer Dennis Rader

JAMES RICHMOND

TABLE OF CONTENTS

DENNIS RADER'S CHILDHOOD AND BACKGROUND

Dennis Lynn Rader's parents, Dorothea and William Rader married and settled down in Pittsburg, Kansas in the early spring of 1941. They were both members of Zion Lutheran Church and their relationship was embraced by their families and considered favorable to both parties. They would remain married until William's death in 1996. William would live during the terror of the "Bind, Torture and Kill [them]" serial killer (BTK) but would die almost ten years before his first-born son would be revealed as the BTK and confess to his crimes—including ten murders.

The BTK's mother, Dorothea, was not as fortunate, as she lived two years into his confession and subsequent incarceration before her death in 2007. Many commented that Dorothea was never able to reconcile the son she loved with the monster he was known to be. Shortly after his arrest in 2005, Dorothea's third-born son, Jeff, said that his mother was in denial and that, like him, she stilled loved Dennis.

It was in their first marital home, in Pittsburg, Kansas, in the spring of 1945 that Dorothea and William's first child was born. They could never foresee his dark infamy. Dennis Lynn Rader, born March 9th, 1945, would be the first of four boys born to the couple. Because his parents were devout Lutherans, Rader was baptized quite young at the Zion Lutheran Church with their family congregation standing as witnesses. Shortly after his baptism, the couple moved their family to 4815 North Seneca Street in Wichita, Kansas, where they remained in the family home until 2005. After Dennis Rader's confession and arrest, the house and the family were receiving too much media attention for the family to handle. They sold the house to escape the notoriety and torrent of public scrutiny.

Dennis Rader's mother, Dorothea, worked long hours in a grocery store called Leekers, and her long hours affected Rader in negative ways. Later in life, he would tell authorities that his mother neglected him as a child. He claimed that he grew resentful of her absence in his young life, claiming he felt "ignored" by her, and confessed to having a grudge against her, saying, "I got along real well with Dad, but Mom wasn't always so happy. I've always loved her. I still love her greatly. But I did have a little –a little bit of a grudge against Momma." But even from prison, he stresses his love for her.

His father, William, worked for the electric company KG&E in early 1948. Between them, the Raders were able to provide a modest but secure financial upbringing for their boys. But these jobs required them to work long hours just to keep the family in a working-class economic status. In order to maintain their modest standard of living, both parents had to sacrifice home life for long hours at work. And this was especially true of his father, William, who was away from home a memorable portion of his childhood.

Despite his dad's absence, Rader focused his discontent toward his mother. According to Rader, even when his mother was at home, she spent her time reading magazines and watching the television, leaving his grandparents to look after him, or, more frequently, leaving him to look after himself. It was his grandmother, in fact, who unknowingly opened up a sexual awareness for Rader.

He remembers, at a very young age, watching her slaughter a chicken for dinner and feeling himself become sexually aroused at the violence of the act and the drawn-out death of the chicken. As the family began to grow and the house became busy with the industry of four young boys, Rader was able to expand his secret sexual life without notice. During his grade school years, Rader joined the Boy Scouts, and this membership would become an important part of his adult life once he had his own son. Indeed, his heavy involvement with the Scouts would one day provide for him an alibi for one of his murders.

Rader tells Dr. Katherine Ramsland, author of *Confession of a Serial Killer: The Untold Story of Dennis Rader, The BTK Killer* that his sexual fantasies were always dark, even from a very young age. Ramsland worked with Rader for six years after his incarceration to gather research for her book. When they heard of the pending publication of her book, all ten of Rader's victims' families petitioned the court to intercede on their behalf to prohibit Rader from profiting from his crimes. A trust was set up to secure a portion of the profits made from any media forum for victim advocacy programs.

But long before he became infamous, Rader began exploring the darker side of his sexual fetishes. He tells Ramsland of an incident that happened early in his childhood when his mother got her ring stuck on one of the sofa springs. The ring was tangled within one of the coils and she couldn't break her hand free from the ring or release the ring from the coil. She panicked. Rader was in the room when she realized she was stuck. He saw that she was terrified, and when turned to her first-born son, begging him to go and get help, Rader told Ramsland that he was sexually aroused at her distress of being trapped. He was excited by her feeling of helplessness. The expression on her face and her emotional fear imprinted on his mind, and he claims he went seeking after that image his entire life.

For example, he began cutting out what he refers to as "slick ads" of attractive women he found in his mother's magazines and pasting the images to index cards. Once affixed to the note card, he would draw binds and gags on the picture, then carry this growing collection around in his pocket. Rader sought to reach sexual climax by envisioning the distressed look of panic on the women's faces. Ramsland worked with Rader for over six years after his arrest and confessions. She patiently gained his trust, but he never fully gained hers. She recognized his narcissistic tendencies and knew that they would prohibit him from true vulnerability. He would share with Ramsland only as much as it would serve him. Rader craved attention and dreamed of fame. He saw Ramsland's book as a way to distinguish himself from the other millions of prisoners locked away from the public's eye or imagination. So, Rader was willing to share intimate details of his crimes with her just so long as she was willing to continue to see him (and more importantly to him, give him attention) and to write about the crimes he was proud of committing.

He admitted to her that once he became aware of his sexual desires after watching his grandmother slaughter the chicken, he also would then become aroused when being spanked. He was not embarrassed by these feelings and certainly was willing to have what some would consider shameful sexual urgings published in a book he knew would be read by a large demographic of the world.

During his grade school years, he developed sexual fantasies involving silos, many of which were found near his home. He called them "castles" and fantasized about capturing a girl and taking her to the castle where he would bind and rape her. He was taken by the imagery of controlling the physical environment as well as the victim herself. Indeed, when he began his murderous lifestyle, controlling the house was his first priority. He confessed that, at his first murder site— where he would assault a mother and her daughter before killing them, in addition to murdering a young boy and the older victim's husband— if they had not complied with him, he wasn't sure if he could have gone through with it. But he had a pistol, and they obeyed his every command. Being in control and then stoking the fear and terror in his victims became a driving force for Rader.

But before he actually began his three decade long murderous career, he limited his sexual arousal and drive to fantasies. He often fantasized about tying women to the train track that ran through the woods he and his brothers hunted and played in. One of his first remembered fantasies, one he recalls with detailed pride, involved Annette Funiculi, a famous Mouseketeer from the original cast of the television show *The Mickey Mouse Club*. This popular show debuted in 1955 when Rader was ten years old and just coming into his own sexual awareness and proclivities. He considered Funiculi one of his first "targets" and spent many hours in his childhood fantasizing about binding and then raping her. When a masturbatory incident especially aroused him, he called it "Sparky Big Time" and referred to his orgasms as "Big G."

In fact, masturbation was his preferred method of sexual gratification. While he would go on to leave semen at some of his crime scenes, he never penetrated his victims. The semen he emitted at the crime scenes was always a result of his masturbatory act at the scene.

Rader was 14 years old when he began secretly reading and masturbating to excerpts from a book his father owned called *Lonely Heart Killers* by Tobin T. Buhk. The book tells the story of Martha Beck and Raymond Fernandez, two murderers who met their victims through Lonely Hearts ads. These newspaper ads allowed singles to post invitations to meet other singles and are considered the origin of the online dating websites available today. In *Lonely Heart Killers,* Tobin details the horror of their murders (eight known victims) including the murder of a young girl after they had murdered her mother. Beck admitted to drowning the girl in a basin of water then burying her in the basement next to her mother, who had been dead for three days. The couple was eventually caught, convicted, and executed.

These stories sexually aroused Rader and helped to increase his knowledge, awareness and vocabulary surrounding sexual assault and murder. As his proclivities grew, he began to experiment with violence in real life, not just in fantasy. It was during his primary school years at Riverview Elementary School in Wichita that he began hanging cats from laundry lines, claiming he became sexually excited watching them squirm and eventually die.

Another serial killer, active during Rader's childhood, inspired Rader in his freshman year of high school. Harvey Glatman, who was executed when Rader was 14, was known as the Lonely Hearts Killer. Rader wanted to become just like him. He studied the newspaper clippings of Glatman's crimes and aspired to emulate him. He considered Glatman an inspiration for who he now knew he wanted to become.

Glatman was twelve years old when his parents became alarmed at his swollen, red neck. He calmly explained to them that when he was in his bath, he had tied a rope around his neck and secured it through the tub drain. He pulled on the rope to suffocate himself as a form of sexual pleasure. His mother, deeply concerned about this aberrant behavior, took Glatman to the family physician, where she was told he would "grow out of this behavior." But, like Rader, who also engaged in asphyxia erotica in his childhood and beyond, Glatman did not grow out of it.

In 1957, when Rader was twelve years old himself, Glatman moved to Los Angeles and began trolling for victims in modeling agencies. Regarded as "safe" and "honorable" by the public, Glatman posed as a photographer and found it easy to lure young women to his apartment where he would tie them up, rape them, and photograph the event. When he finished with his protracted sexual assaults, he would strangle his victims. Glatman buried their bodies in the desert.

He was caught when his fourth victim—putting up a valiant struggle—caught the eye of a police officer in the middle of the attempted kidnapping. The officer arrested Glatman on suspicion of kidnapping, and while in custody, Glatman happily confessed to the murders of his three previous victims. He led police to a toolbox where he stored the photos of the sexual assaults and murders. Glatman's willingness to discuss his crimes—even the pride he exhibited in his confessions—would be mirrored by Rader at his own public confession in February of 2005. Both Rader and Glatman shared the narcissistic trait of craving public attention—they dreamed of receiving accolades for their cleverness in committing the murders.

Rader himself confessed to his attachment and idolization of Glatman. He adored the photos of Glatman's victims being gagged and bound. When Rader sketched his final victim, Dolores Davis, with a look of horror on her face at the moment of her death, it was a silent tribute to his hero, Harvey Glatman.

At the time of Rader's arrest, he was the president of the counsel of the congregation at his Lutheran church. Like Glatman, he was not considered threatening by the community, and was even considered honorable. Bob Beatty, an author who is often credited for bringing Rader back into the limelight after a long hiatus of murdering, says of the police at the time, "They were looking for Crazy Charles Manson, somebody with a history of crimes, sex crimes and mental disorders. You get on the elevator with Charles Manson and you are going to move to the other side of the elevator. You get on the elevator with the BTK and you are going to smile, nod and have a conversation. You're never going to suspect this guy."

Indeed, Rader's "honorable" lifestyle as church leader, husband and even Scout leader led many in his circle to be astonished at the time of his arrest. Denise Maddox was a coworker of Rader's when he worked at the security firm, a place in which he was employed for fourteen years. He claimed he used the job to help him search for victims; homeowners, often women, would invite him into their houses, where he would sketch, with notable detail, the layout of their homes.

It was during his employment with this security firm when he sexually assaulted and strangled Nancy Fox. Because the press weren't writing about it, he knew that her body had not yet been discovered. So Rader called the police, leaving a 14 second message alerting them to the homicide at Nancy Fox's address. The media played the recording multiple times during the news. Maddox, Rader's coworker, heard the recording but never associated Rader, her office mate, with the voice. In an interview with CBS News, she later said, "I was working with all these guys, sharing a restroom with them. I was the only woman and he [Rader] always wanted to make sure they put the toilet seat down and no dirty jokes."

Rader learned how to operate between his two worlds, in part, by studying Glatman. But in his younger years, before he began assaulting and killing women and then the male witnesses to his crimes, he followed Glatman's playbook with precision. He was careful about hiding his sexual arousal at what would be considered inappropriate stimuli—for Rader, things like being spanked, watching a chicken get its head cut off, and pornographic cartoon images of women being bound and controlled.

In the 1960's Rader began attending Pleasant Valley Middle School. His younger brothers, Paul (born 1947), Jeff (born 1955), and Bill (born 1959), were old enough to play with now, and the boys frequently went out into the woods to hunt and fish. By all accounts, the brothers enjoyed a close sibling relationship perhaps fostered by the unsupervised play they enjoyed as young boys.

It is notable that when Rader began sending letters to taunt the police regarding his unsolved murders, he used the name Bill in the signature line. Whether or not this was a nod toward his youngest brother is not known.

Rader signed the letters Bill Thomas Killman and then in parenthesis wrote "BTK." But Rader would give himself multiple aliases over the years including, The Wichita Strangler, The Poetic Strangler, The Asphyxiator, The Garrot Phantom, The Bondage Strangler and The Wichita Hangman.

Long into his incarceration and shortly after his daughter, Kerri (nee Rader) Rawson released her highly publicized memoir, *A Serial Killer's Daughter: My Story of Faith, Love and Overcoming*, he reached out to the media from his prison cell. Perhaps jealous of his daughter's public attention, he offered the media the names of the two demons he claimed resided in him and prodded him to commit his crimes. He named them as "Batter" and "Factor X." Factor X was not a new revelation. When he worked with Ramsland for six years at the commencement of his confinement, he spoke to her of Factor X, but "Batter" seemed to be a new addition to his story.

Ramsland wrote that Rader only agreed to work with her in order to discover whatever it was in him that caused him to "go dark," as he called it. Rader offered that this element was called "Factor X." Ramsland writes that, "Factor X is less of a mystery than Rader imagines." She argues that Factor X, something she calls a *trajectory toward violence* is much simpler than Rader would allow. She sees this trajectory as a confluence of "unique sexual impulses, desire for fame, and delusions of a spy-like double life intersecting with his fantasy life." She adds that the final element in this trajectory was the very unglamorous notion of his "opportunity to commit the murders." In other words, he had the time.

In this analysis, Ramsland all but refutes Rader's hypothesis of a mysterious, special ingredient that made him behave in the way that he did. Ramsland argues that Rader needed this Factor X to be enigmatic. She says, "He doesn't like that it's not that hard. He wants to it be this intense, deep mystery that no one will ever quite access."

It is likely Rader invented mysterious demons in himself because he needed to set himself apart from ordinary people. He was always proud of his accomplishments as a serial killer. Ramsland concedes that, "I don't think he told me everything and I don't think he always told me the truth." But she is confident that her trajectory theory is a reasonable, if not as salacious as Rader's explanation for his own deviant behavior. Ramsland believes that despite his false claims and braggadocio, she, "got Rader pretty well."

When the boys were grade school-aged children and long before Rader named his secret specialness "Factor X," they had free reign of a large forest area near their house where they spent their free time playing and hunting. It was an ideal spot for children to play and explore—except for the fact that Rader was interested in the killing turtles there and claimed to enjoy stabbing them to death.

Rader remained close to his brothers into his adulthood. When he was arrested nearly forty-five years after their idyllic childhood memories, they stood by his innocence until he confessed. Even then, they had a very difficult time reconciling the older brother they knew and loved as a monster, capable of such destruction and pain. Rader's younger brother, Jeff, spoke with the press after Dennis Rader's arrest. He said he just couldn't believe that his brother was the BTK. When the police told him his brother's true identity, he said, "I laughed at them," telling them, "there is NO way. You've got the wrong guy."

Later in the day, speaking from behind a screen porch door at the family home and learning his brother had confessed to the crimes, it seemed reality was beginning to sink in for him. "It's too hard on my mother," he said. "My mother still can't believe it. She's still very much in denial. So am I. But maybe the reality is starting to creep in."

Jeff Rader's mother asked to visit her son after his arrest but her request, and then later, Jeff's requests, were denied by the police. This set of circumstances points to a meaningful and relevant relationship shared among the family. Jeff stated, "I don't think my brother is the BTK, but if he is, if that's the truth, then let the truth be the truth and may God have mercy on his soul." This statement may point to his slow acceptance of his brother's crimes. But even within that acknowledgment, his little brother offers his brother, the serial killer, the compassion of mercy.

Rader used his middle school years to practice and expand his torture and killing of animals. But it was also during this age range that he turned his attention to humans. He began to "troll" (as he called it) women and girls in his neighborhood. He was already skilled at hanging cats to watch their prolonged deaths, and he had begun stabbing turtles and torturing forest animals. But perhaps these activities no longer provided him with the sexual exhilaration he desired. He would need to escalate his behavior.

And so, he began his life as a voyeur during this time, often standing outside his neighbor's houses in the dark, watching the neighborhood women and girls undress through their un-curtained windows. By the time he attended high school, he was already stealing undergarments from his neighbors' laundry lines. Then, later, he accelerated the thrill by breaking into their homes and stealing the undergarments from their dresser drawers. He began wearing this stolen female underwear as a form of sexual arousal. He would hide these stolen items in what he referred to as "hidey holes" which included burial sites in the forest, secured hidden spots under bridges, secret hiding places inside his home and, most surprisingly, church.

Once he began to murder his victims, he continued this practice of creating hidey holes to stash souvenirs stolen from his victims' houses. And he also began varying the trophies he collected from simply stealing their intimate undergarments, to taking their driver's licenses, jewelry, and work identification cards. He especially liked any memento that contained the victim's name and picture. He created so many "hidey holes" for his trophies that when he was finally captured, even he was unable to remember all the locations of the hidden stashes.

By high school, he also began experimenting on himself with erotic asphyxiation by tightening ropes around his neck to the point of passing out, then loosening the ropes during masturbation. One of his favorite erotic spots was a local cattle tank used to water the cows. He would tie himself to the tank and masturbate there in the field. He remembers that during this time, his mother beat him with a belt. He cannot remember the offense he was being punished for, but he did remember that he was sexually aroused during the beating.

It was during his high school years that he became obsessed over the number three, although how that obsession played out in his later murders remains unclear. But Rader is clear with the fact the by the time he graduated from high school, he considered himself an accomplished "hunter" or "predator."

While attending Wichita Heights Valley Center High School he became dissatisfied with the pseudo sexual erotica he found available to him in print, so he began creating his own. Rader had become a big fan of The New Detective magazines (also his father's) which depicted cartoon pictures of women in sexualized restraints. But the magazines soon bored Rader, so he began to draw his own collection which he used as sexual aids during masturbation.

He began to separate aspects of his personality. For example, in high school, he was described as a quiet and polite student. He mostly kept to himself and there is no record of his membership in any of the high school clubs or organizations. One former classmate commented that he had "no interest in modern music" and that he had "no sense of humor." He was considered studious and focused. This focus, however, did not result in good grades. Rader graduated with a low C average, and this lackluster academic performance would follow him into college. Rader admitted in an interview that he was a bad student and terrible with spelling and grammar.

Despite the low grades, he developed the keen skill to present an under-the-radar persona at school and church while compartmentalizing his deviant and criminal persona. In fact, once he was finally captured some forty years later, a famous headline read "Rader kept under the radar."

To view the entirety of Rader's childhood and contrast it to his remarkable reign as a serial killer is to immerse oneself in an ongoing philosophical debate regarding what creates a serial killer. Peter Vronsky, historian and author, tackles this complicated issue in his book *Sons of Cain: The History of Serial Killers from the Stone Age to the Present*. When asked if serial killers are born or made, he believes the question may be too reductive. In other words, he doesn't know. He writes that he believes, "it's intrinsic to the human survival mechanism that we have this capacity to repeatedly kill." He then offers a more controversial argument stating, "Perhaps it's not that serial killers are made, but that the majority of us are unmade by good parenting and socialization." Vronsky's belief is not well accepted in mainstream society. He is suggesting that all humans are born with a bit of monster blood flowing through their infant arms and it is 0nly through positive societal influences and proper parenting that this monster element is tamed.

More to his point, he is suggesting that rather than question if serial killers are a product of nature (evil from birth) or nurture (evil due to experience) is the wrong question to be asking. He believes that all humans are born with the capacity to become serial killers. He sees the refinement of humans who grow up *not* to be serial killers as the inverse answer to the question regarding the origin of these societal monsters. When reduced to its lowest form, Vronksy sees all humans as being born monstrous (among other good qualities, as well) and that experience (nurture) smooths away these sharp fangs of darkness into ordinary, compliant, empathetic creatures. Ultimately, he eschews the idea that all serial killers suffered severe trauma in their childhoods.

Indeed, Rader's childhood has remained under hyper-scrutiny since his arrest. Some experts argue that while he claims a "happy, normal childhood," he must be lying about the normalcy; how can a well-trained child from a well-respected home become such an aberrant member of society? Psychologist and professor, Dr. Terence G. Leary, remains dubious at Rader's "picture perfect childhood." He believes there are uncovered secrets in Rader's childhood that could reveal why or how he became the BTK.

In an interview, Leary argues that "Rader's methods of torture and murder are signs of someone who was regularly exposed to horrific abuse." But Vransky counters this argument by stating, "It's true that almost all serial killers suffered childhood trauma. But here's the problem: if 100 kids grow up in an abusive foster home, and one turns out to be a serial killer – what about the other 99? They grew up to be, well, maybe not all well-adjusted citizens, but certainly not serial killers. What is the missing X factor?"

And Leary can see his point. He says, "Dennis Rader has been an enigma to many of us in the field because I don't think the people who claim to be experts are, regarding Dennis, and I'll tell you why. They say he was the squeaky clean, oldest of four boys, very traditional parents, traditional family, went to school, did the right things etcetera, so there were no clues."

But Leary argues that there were clues, hidden clues. He suggests looking more closely at Rader's propensity toward animal cruelty. He believes Rader's actions against animals prove a hidden abuse in his childhood. He states, "He [Rader] was terribly to cruel to animals. He also engaged in mutilations of some degree. He would torture to a large degree his victims — all 10 of them — intense torture — really, really, cruel torture — and he would get some close to death and then revive them so they could live this horrific experience again, and he would do that simultaneously. It's not only a very evil heinous act but it is driven by someone who is exposed to horrific abuse, so something is hidden here. This is a puzzle…not all is meeting the eye here."

While Leary points to culpability resting in the childhood home and whatever abuse the serial killer endured there, Vransky argues that the onus of responsibility lay on the perpetrator's shoulders only. He says, "My sense here is that the responsibility falls on the offender here. Serial killers choose to act upon their compulsions.

In Rader's case, his childhood has been esteemed as an enviable one by experts and family members alike. Rader himself, although known to lie to protect his ego, speaks fondly of his childhood. He claims he was happy growing up with brothers and that he loves his parents. Indeed, he proclaimed love for his mother on the night of his arrest.

The Center for Crime and Justice Studies believe serial killers like Rader are created by a convergence of several societal factors, including mass urbanization, which they claim produces a "society of strangers." This theoretically makes predatory killing much easier and less detectable due to lack of familial and neighborhood ties. But Rader may have belied this finding when he murdered Marin Hedge, his neighbor just several doors down. He not only sexually assaulted and then strangled her, but he then brought her body to his Lutheran church where he displayed her in graphic sexual poses under the choir robes in the vestry. This crime was considered the most personal of his victims, but Rader claims to have felt no more regard for her than the others. But the fact that he killed her within an intimate circle of his own life would suggest that mass urbanization may not have been a factor in Rader's inoculation from a "regular" boy into notorious serial killer.

The Center for Criminal Justice adds another tenent they believe assists in the making of serial killers, and here, Rader may well fit into their argument. They claim that "mass media and the culture of celebrity" help to encourage would-be serial killers into action. This is arguably true for Rader's childhood experiences. The argument can be made that the celebrity of the Lonely Hearts Killers and Harvey Glatman offered Rader inspiration and guidance. He openly claims an affinity for them and others. In one of his taunting messages to the police department, he refers to Ted Bundy and David Berkowitz (The Son of Sam). Rader's fascination with serial killing and the celebrity of the killers themselves could have pushed Rader to seek the same kind of inglorious attention.

The MacDonald Triad was published during Rader's childhood in 1963. Rader was 13 years old when this controversial research gained public attention. Psychiatrist J.M. MacDonald published the MacDonald Triad which argues that there are three common denominator traits that can be found in all serial killers' childhoods, which are:

Being cruel or abusive to animals, especially pets

Setting fire to objects or otherwise committing other acts of arson

Regularly wetting the bed

Rader, of course, does not fit the MacDonald Triad in that he only connects to the first of the three requirements for childhood tells. MacDonald agrees that many people experience all three categories of behaviors in his triad and do not grow up to be serial killers. He also conceded that some serial killers do not fall inside his triad of behavioral constructs. But with Rader in particular, and serial killers in general, scientists' urge to analyze childhood traits to then predict anti-social behavior is a long-standing tradition.

Society needs to understand how to identify a serial killer before he (or, more rarely, she) can infect the population. A serial killer is a known predator putting the general population in danger. And serial killers like Rader, with his innocuous assimilation into culture, including "safe" environments like church and boy scouts, cause real terror within the fabric of a normalized society. Rader himself said he was willing to work with Dr. Ramsland in order to help others identify "wolves in sheep's clothing." Of course, Ramsland adds that Rader agreed to work with her to keep himself in the public eye to remain relevant and publicly talked about.

Despite theories that Rader faced childhood abuse, evidence weighs heavily on a typical upbringing inside a loving, family home. Rader was able to maintain close relationships with both of his brothers, and aside from him using the baby brother's name in a taunt to police (Bill Thomas Killman, BTK) neither Rader, nor any of his brothers, claim any kind of cruel treatment or unusual circumstances in their childhood that could predict such dire outcomes for so many lives. All that remains clear is that Rader's predilection for sexual arousal centered around the misery, distress, and control of others, and that this predilection formed organically as he grew into a sexual, salient human.

Rader's young adult life would begin inauspiciously. He would give himself a two-year gap before attending college. After his high school graduation in 1963, he remained living in the family home and followed in his mother's footsteps by working at the local grocery store. There is little information about this time in his life, and Rader never refers to this time as anything full of angst or doubt. But he was a young man on the cusp of independence, and so one might assume he held some frustration at having to live at home and to work in his mother's place of employment.

Additionally, not much is made of his short tenure as a meat butcher. This is perhaps because Rader did not stab, cut, or otherwise mutilate his victims. His mode of murder was prolonged strangulation—with the notable exception of a victim's brother, who was able to escape despite Rader shooting a bullet through his chest. Rader would bring the gun to the crime scene only to gain control of his victims; all of them complied because of the gun. He himself expressed surprise at how easy it was to control a room full of people (when referring to the Otero family murders). He said that once they saw the gun, they did whatever he told them to do. But unlike other known serial killers, Rader's experience as a meat cutter did not appear to overlap into the murderous section of his life.

Rader maintained his habits of "trolling" by prowling the neighborhood at night to either commit voyeurism or to break into homes he had already scanned to steal pieces of their intimate apparel. He continued this behavior even during his courtship with his wife, Paula. At his sentencing hearing Rader claimed he was "always trolling. It never really stopped."

In 1965, Rader enrolled in Kansas Wesleyan University in Selena, Kansas. This school was far away from his home in Wichita, so he moved out on his own to attend school. He lasted two semesters there, dropping out in 1966 due to poor grades. It remains unknown if his parents refused him a place back in the family home, but once he dropped out of college, he enrolled in the military in the summer of 1966 on August 17. It's likely that his father, a marine veteran himself, may have influenced his decision to join the military. Rader certainly esteemed his father and saw him as a man to look up to. Rader may consider it fortunate that his father died before his son's true identity was revealed to the world. But whatever the influences, Dennis Rader, at age 21, became a member of the United States Air Force.

For his basic training, Rader was shipped to Lackland Airforce Base in San Antonio, Texas. This would be the farthest he lived away from his parents. He stayed in Texas for a year, when he was stationed at Brookley Air Force Base in Mobile, Alabama early in 1966. Again, common among military personnel, Rader was moved around frequently. By the following year, in January of 1968, Rader was assigned to Kadena Air Force Base in Okinawa, an island off the coast of and belonging to Japan. From there the moves became more frequent. During the course of his enlistment, he would live in Japan, Korea, Greece and Turkey until his discharge on August 11, 1970.

Rader was one of many serial killers who served in the military. He is joined in this odd convergence by other notable serial killers as David

Berkowitz (one of Rader's personal heroes) who served in the US Army in South Korea and received an honorable discharge. Jeffrey Dahmer served in the Army and was deployed to Germany as a medical technician. He was released from service due to his alcoholism. Dean Corll (aka The Candy Man) was drafted into the US Army in 1967 until he was honorably discharged. He would go on to abduct, torture, rape and murder 28 boys before he was caught. And finally, Gary Ridgeway joins the infamous club by serving in the Navy on a supply ship. Ridgeway enrolled in the Navy the same year Rader was discharged: 1970. There are no studies published to align serial killers and military service, but it's worth noting that these five men all served the country with honor only to ravage that country with fear and terror once they were discharged from service.

And Rader was an exemplary soldier. As with his high school career, he stayed inconspicuous and accomplished what was asked of him. Rader, like the other serial killers in this loosely associated club, was discharged honorably with an unremarkable service record. Inside the Air Force, he worked as an installer of antenna equipment and was considered "one of the guys." He reached the rank of sergeant and would later be called "regular soldier" as an active-duty airman. His former military friends were shocked when he confessed to being the Bind Torture Kill (BTK) serial killer in 2005. He did excel in in marksmanship, earning the Small Arms Expert Marksmanship Ribbon during his enlisted time. There is no record of Rader committing any crimes during his military career, but Rader himself states that even though he didn't commit his first murder until 1974, he was always "trolling" and constantly "surveilling."

These statements can lead to the belief that he continued to stalk and enter women's homes through-out his military service. Perhaps his basic training provided him with more professional tools to use for incognito surveillance, as he was never discovered—or if he was discovered, he was never reported during his active-duty years.

Rader moved back to Wichita, Kansas after his discharge, but would serve in the reserves for two more years in his hometown. Initially, he moved back home with his parents, but once he began a courtship with one of the church girls, he finally moved into his own apartment in Wichita. He eventually married Paula Dietz (born May 5, 1948) after an acceptable courtship period. They were married at the Lutheran church on May 22, 1971. She would remain married to him for 34 years, divorcing him in an "emergency divorce" that was hastily approved by a judge after Rader's arrest. The divorce was final only a few months after Rader's arrest on July 27, 2005. Throughout their marriage, she worked as a bookkeeper and volunteered at the church with her husband. After his arrest, Dietz never visited him in prison, nor did she attend any of his hearings or sentencing.

But before the horrors of her husband's secret life were revealed to her and the world, the couple enjoyed a happy marriage. They both had attended Wichita Heights High School together, and they both were active within the Lutheran church. However, Dietz didn't meet Rader in church or in high school, but rather at Leekers' grocery where he cut meat and she shopped. Dietz attended the American University of Wichita, earning her degree in bookkeeping. She maintained a close relationship with her parents throughout her marriage. Her mother worked as a librarian and her father as a car engineer.

Originally, Paula and Rader moved into a one-story apartment on Independence Street in Wichita but, possibly due to lack of work opportunities, they moved to the nearby town of Park City, Kansas.

Rader was 26 and his wife Paula was 23. He spent his time working as the meat cutter at Leeker's, and his wife worked as a bookkeeper. They both were involved with the church, and Paula volunteered there and sang in the choir.

Rader soon grew dissatisfied with his meat cutting job. Even as young child, Rader preferred the outdoors and soon began to look for work that didn't require him to be trapped inside. He eventually found work in one of Wichita's largest employers, the Coleman Company, that manufactured camping supplies. Two of his future victims also worked at Coleman: Julie Ortero and Kathyrn Bright. It is generally accepted that they caught his attention inside the Coleman plant and that he targeted each of them as a potential victim or what he called "projects." But his attacks on these women would not occur until after he left his employment at Coleman in July of 1973. Additionally, Rader never confessed to making them his "targets" while they were all employed at the Coleman plant.

After some time at the plant, Rader felt himself once again feeling bored and dissatisfied with his work. He continued at the Coleman plant but complained that he found the work unfulfilling and dull. Shortly after starting the job at Coleman, Rader enrolled in Butler County Community College in El Dorado, Kansas and went on to earn an Associate's degree in electronics. Rader considered himself a poor student who hovered just above a D average. He struggled with dyslexia which made him a poor speller.

This spelling issue would eventually lead to one of the confirmations of his identity as the BTK Killer. Many of the taunting notes he would leave for police and with media stations contained misspelled words. Analysts would spend hours poring over his letters, looking for codification of his spelling mistakes, thinking he may be leaving coded messages through them. The BTK Killer enjoyed leaving codes and hidden messages for the police. But once he was caught, he confessed to simply being a poor speller.

Three months after getting his Associate's degree and leaving Coleman, in September of 1973, Rader enrolled in Wichita State University to study criminal justice. His wife, Paula, by this time had already graduated with her Bachelor of Science in bookkeeping, and perhaps he felt jealous of her accomplishments. As with his scholastic work at Butler Community College, he struggled with his grades at the four-year state school. It would take him six years to complete the two years remaining for him to earn his bachelor's degree. However, it's notable that Rader only took night classes and maintained full time employment throughout the entirety of his college education.

After leaving Coleman and starting school, Rader found employment with an airplane company called Cessna which manufactured airplanes. He was only employed with them a few months when they fired him. He claims that it was this demoralizing circumstance of being fired that led him to troll and then "target" Julie Otero (33) and Josephina Otero (11).

Rader's life is difficult to comprehend; there is a dramatic difference between his "normal" persona of husband, church leader, and father, and his now-famous three decades long stint as a serial killer. Rader explains this disparity by compartmentalizing his life into sections he calls "cubes." The cube containing his childhood and young adolescent life, he refers to as "The Minotoar." In Greek mythology, the Minotoar has the body of a human male and the head of bull. The Minotoar made its living by devouring the sacrificial humans who were thrown into the Labyrinth which was a dungeon-maze type of structure that was buried under King Mino's castle. Despite having a male body, the Minotaur was a considered a monster. He was later killed by Theseus who vowed to his father, King Aegeus that he would descend into the Labyrinth to kill the Minotaur in a mission to save the children and those coming in later generations who may find themselves sacrificed into the Labyrinth, only to be devoured by the bogeyman who resided there: the Minotaur.

King Aegeus begged his son not to embark on such a dangerous journey, fearing he would be become a victim to the monster, but Prince Theseus successfully slaughtered the Minotaur by varying accounts of using a sword, a club, or his bare hands. But all historic accounts agree that once he killed the Minotaur, he led the surviving Athenians out of the Labyrinth and sailed safely away from Crete.

Rader's self-identification with the Minotaur strikes some mental health professionals as an acknowledgment that, even in his "Minotaur Cube," Rader recognized that he was a monster who must be slain to be stopped. Later in his life, Rader would rely on these "cubed" compartmentalizations to explain his "regular life" from what he termed "going dark."

THE MURDERS

THE OTERO FAMILY

Shortly after being fired by Cessna, and in the cold Kansas winter, on January 15 ,1974, Rader committed his first murders. Rader had focused his attention on Mrs. Julia Marie Otero and her twelve-year-old daughter, Josephina. Rader, constantly on patrol for victims, targeted Mrs. Otero and began stalking her several months before the event. Rader refers to the stages serial killers go through when amping up to a murder. After the trolling stage he would settle on a "target" and after the target was selected, he moved them into the "project" phase. This involved hours, sometimes months, of surveillance and general snooping to determine the lifestyle and habits of his "project." In Mrs. Otero's case, it remains undetermined if he targeted her as a project back when they were both employed at Colemans, of if he saw her by chance on one of his trolling sessions. But what is clear is that he confessed that he did "maliciously, intentionally, with premeditation, kill Joseph Otero." This crime, his first, is considered to be his most heinous. Although it would not be the only crime with multiple victims, it would be the crime with the most victims killed at one time.

When asked by Judge Gregory L. Waller, Judge of Division 5, of the 18 Judicial Circuit on June 27, 2005 why he chose this particular family, Rader answered nonplussed.

Judge: This particular location, did you know these people?

Rader: No, that's—that was part of my-I guess what you call fantasy.

These people were selected.

Judge: All right, so you were engaged in some kind of fantasy during this period of time?

Rader: Yes, sir.

Judge: All right, now when you use the term "fantasy," is this something you were doing for your personal pleasure?

Rader: Sexual fantasy, sir.

Rader tells the court in his official confession that he had a basic plan "in the back of his mind" of what he intended to do.

In a later interview from prison, with NBC's Dateline production crew, Rader provides more insight into how he chose the Otero family.

"That neighbor, I guess, what I call a haunt. It had a special appeal to it." He tells the interviewer that he began to "know the people" and to write down phone numbers and addresses. He says that "Edgemoor was my first big haunt."

He says he chose the house for multiple reasons. The first being that Julie Otero "caught his eye." He began following her as she drove her morning school run. The Otero's had five children in several different schools. He said he began to fantasize about "the project." He liked the location of a corner house and considered it "a possibility."

Rader: "I was between work. Idle hands, what is it?

Mendoza (NBC): "the devil's workshop?"

Rader: "Yes, and all these things seem to happen when I had idle hands.

All these things seem to happen when I have idle hands. I had lost a job at Cessna and that was demoralizing to me."

Rader continues to press that it was Julie Otero, the thirty-three-year-old wife and mother who caught his attention, but when Mendoza asks, why her specifically, Rader quietly adds, "Mrs. Otero's attractive. And then I saw Josephine (11) too. So I must have had that somewhere in my mind. A younger person. That must have locked into my mind." From this confession, it appears evident that Josephina was the target of his crime. And this can further be substantiated by examining the events inside the actual crime itself.

Sometime between 7 and 7:30 a.m., Rader approached 1834 Edgemoor Street, the Otero's house, that he had been surveilling and stalking for some time. He expected to find Mrs. Julie Otero and her twelve-year old daughter, Josephina, at home as he had watched the family's daily school routine for some amount of time. What surprised him was that Mr. Joseph Otero was home. An additional surprise was the family dog, whose name holds weighted irony. The Otero's named their dog Lucky.

Rader said he cut the phone line, which, at that time, was an actual, physical line that ran from each house to a local receptor. Rader committed his crimes in an age before cell phones and fiberoptics. Nearly every home in this era had what was referred to as a "land-line." His cutting of the phone line would become part of Rader's modus operandi before entering each of his victim's homes. This was more than just compulsive behavior—this was Rader fully understanding that what he was doing was criminal and that he intended to control, dominate, and terrorize the household by cutting off their one avenue of conceptual escape: their ability to phone 911 for help. So, on this murder, his first, he cut the phone cord and then hesitated at the back door.

Mendoza: Were you nervous?

Rader: Oh, extremely nervous. All of sudden, and it's funny, I had already cut the phone line because I left my knife; I left my cutter. I had to go back and get those later. But then the door opened. So, here I am. Do I just walk out the back door and they call the police? Or do I go for it? I went for it. You know, it's just like, now I can't back out of it. And that's basically what happened all the way through. I can't back out of this. I've got to go all the way through now.

He claims he "had reservations about even going or just walking away, but pretty soon the door opened and I was in." Rader confessed that he entered the home just as Junior (Joseph II, a nine-year-old boy) was leaving with his dad to go to school. As the boy tried to exit the house, Rader stepped in front of him and pushed his way inside. He also claims that at this point, he was motivated by sexual fantasy, that murder was not part of this game.

Rader said that the family didn't take him seriously at first. Mr. Joseph Otero, in fact, thought Rader's presence there was a joke. "Mr. Otero actually stepped up and I told him I was coming for some food. I was wanted in California or wanted. I needed some food and water and some money and transportation. That was my ruse to kind of calm him down. He kind of laughed a little bit. He said, "What is this, a joke? You know, who sent you over? My brother-in-law?"

The family dog was excited by the intrusion and began barking loudly. This barking alarmed Rader, who was afraid the dog would attract the neighbor's attention. He had his pistol drawn and so the family very quickly agreed to obey his requests. Rader claimed he told them he was on the run, that he was a "wanted man" and needed them to give him their car and some food.

He forced Mr. Otero to lie down on the living floor, but Lucky was going wild by this point. Rader later says, "the dog was a real problem, so I, I asked Mr. Otero if he could get the dog out. Mr. Otero was lying on the living floor with his nine-year-old son, Joseph, his eleven-year-old daughter, Josephine and his wife, Julie, all watching in slow-motion horror. Had they united and offered him resistance, Rader says he would have fled. But they remained compliant during the entire ordeal. And the ordeal was to be a lengthy one. Mr. Otero instructed Junior to let the dog out into the backyard, which he did. When Junior returned to the living room, Rader escorted the four family members down the hall to the back bedroom. There, he tied them up.

At his sentencing hearing, Judge Waller challenges Rader's rendition of this sequence. He asks Rader, in response to Rader claiming he has them at gun point "[you tied them up] while still holding them at gunpoint?" To which Rader responds with a laugh, "Well, in between tying, I guess. You know."

Rader says that once the family was bound, they enjoyed a casual conversation but of course, Rader, the narcissist, is the only member of that room alive to tell the story. And he chooses to soften his image by suggesting he was a kind and attentive intruder. By Rader's account, the family encouraged him to take the car and whatever money they had. Rader mentioned that "they didn't have a lot of money." But this conversational period must have gone on for some length of notable time, because Rader says the family members began to complain about their restraints. He says he "re-loosened the bonds a couple of times and tried to make Mr. Otero as comfortable as possible."

Mr. Otero allegedly told Rader that he had recently suffered from a cracked rib from a car accident. Apparently, the manner in which he was bound, and how he was forced lie on the ground, caused his injuries distress. Rader, in an attempt to paint himself a savior of sorts, says he, "had him put a pillow down on his—for his head..." One presumes that Mr. Otero was lying on the floor due to Rader's instructions to "pull a pillow down." But Rader goes a step further to secure the comfort of his targeted murder victim. He tells the court that he, "had him put a parka or coat underneath him." Rader, attempting to explain his momentary compassion for Mr. Otero's distress, says that he's "not a bad guy, I care for people, you know, I have concerns for people."

Now, the family is still relatively calm at this point. They quietly talked to him from their positions as captives. They told him to take the car and go. Rader claimed in court that it was during this time of the family bound and held by gunpoint in a back bedroom that he made his decision to "go ahead and put 'em down—strangle them I guess." Rader wasn't wearing a mask, and because the family could identify him, he knew he must leave no witnesses.

But Rader's claim of a last -minute decision to kill the family goes against later interviews he would give to the media. When he told NBC's Mendoza that he had looked into Josephina's age and what pleasure that might bring him, he lacks any sort of disorganized, chaotic kind of last-minute decision to kill the family. He planned to kill them. Indeed, their murder is what motivated him to enter their lives in the first place.

Mr. Joseph Otero was the first to be murdered. Rader had positioned the family in such a way as to have the males on the floor and the females on the bed. All of them were restrained. Rader says, "Both their hands and their feet were tied up." Rader had already made the decision to kill the males in the room. Mr. Otero, the biggest threat to Rader, was the first to die. Rader said he, "put a plastic bag over his head and then some cords, then tightened it." What Rader omits in his astonishing confession is that he, himself, brought the supplies needed to perform this torture and murder. He called his supply bag his "hit kit," and inside were plastic bags (the kind used at grocery stores), cords, a box cutter and a knife. He came prepared, like a proper Boy Scout, to execute these murders for his sexual gratification. When the judge asks him if Joseph Otero died from Rader's efforts, he answers "no."

Judge Waller: Was this in the bedroom?

Rader: Yes, sir.

Waller: Okay, did he, in fact, suffocate and die as a result of this?

Rader: Not right away, no, sir, he didn't.

Rader said in a later interview with NBC that after he placed the bag over his neck and pulled up on it, "that's when it all hit the fan." The family was watching their beloved husband and father being strangled to death, and it was too much to bear. Their sorrow and horror overcame their fear. Rader said the family "could all see what I was doing." He said the kids "were watching it. They were screaming and hollering."

All the noise and disruption panics Rader. He doesn't like loud noises, as evidenced by his request that the family let Lucky out to the back garden because he was barking so loudly. And now the children are screaming, and Rader knows he must "get control." He continues: "It was really noisy—they were all screaming, and the noise was bothering me. And the mailman would be out there, or somebody would be walking by, so I had to control it very quickly."

Rader knows that once he killed Mr. Otero, he must kill them all. He sighs in his interview with NBC's Mendoza, "[sigh] It was just something I had to do, once I started with Mr. Otero, I knew I had to do all four of 'em. It's like an execution—you know, once you start it, if there's witnesses, you had to do it all the way around."

In this confession in front of Judge Waller, Rader then shifts topic to Mrs. Otero's murder so his admission to this slow strangulation of Mr. Otero goes without further probing. But it must be noted that Joseph's wife, and his two children, were in the room, helplessly watching as Rader murdered their father. And his first attempt at strangulation was unsuccessful, but Rader was in no hurry. One of the reasons he came here was to feel the arousal that he felt certain strangulation would give him. That Joseph's children were bound, crying and terrorized, that his wife lay on the bed listening to her husband struggle inside the plastic bag—these conditions only elevated Rader's pleasure. When the judge asks Rader what happens next, he cheerfully replies,

Rader: Well, after that, I-I did Mrs. Otero. I had never strangled anyone before so I didn't know how much pressure you had to put on a person or how long it would take, but...

Waller: Was she also tied up there in the bedroom?

Rader: Yes. Uh huh...she was on the bed...

Judge Waller interrupts Rader's reveille by inquiring about the children. Perhaps he, like the entire gallery, hoped that the children did not witness their father's murder.

Waller: Where were the children?

Rader: Well, Josephine was on the bed and Junior was on the floor...at this time.

So, no, the children nor their mother were spared the horror of playing witness to their much-loved father and husband's murder. But, of course, this was the way Rader liked it. He needed his audience to be terrified, petrified even, of what Rader forced them to participate in. Rader had told detectives about one of his first, powerful sexual arousals that manifested around the terrified look his mother had on her face when her ring bound her hand to a sofa coil. She was frantic and the more frightened, the more hysterical she became, the more sexually stimulated he became. His game was always terror. It's why he chose strangulation. He and he alone was in complete control of every aspect of another human. And this excited him. He could, and often did, strangle, then release his victim to gasp for breath only to strangle them again. So his murder of Joseph Otero in the cramped bedroom with his own children and wife as witness? It only provided a sexual stimulus that increased as he methodically murdered the family, up until he reached his intended victim, 11-year-old Josephina, who, by this time, would have been shocked and horrified, having suffered through the three murders of her family. Again, Rader murdered them in a particular order to serve his needs.

But Judge Waller is dissatisfied with Rader's rendition. Rader, in his confession, seems to be racing through the events to get to Josephina, but the judge slows him down.

Waller: Can you tell me what happened in regards to Joseph Otero?

Rader: He moved over real quick-like and I think I tore a hole in his bag and I could tell he was having some problems there…

Rader's reference to "some problems there" refers to Joseph's problems in not dying on Rader's terms. Of course, Joseph was having some problems breathing—that was the point of the strangulation. But Otero's struggles become an issue for Rader. He wanted a clean kill. He wanted complete control of the murder scene. Rader tells the judge that once Otero's bag ripped, allowing him access to oxygen, "the whole family just went, they went panicked on me. So, I-I-I worked pretty quick." Justice Waller asks Rader to explain what he means by working "pretty quick." Rader obliges by saying, "Well, I mean, I-I-I strangled Mrs. Otero and then she went out or passed out. I thought she was dead." Rader is very excited in the telling. He is rushing to the part he wants to relive that has him taking Josephina downstairs for a private torture session. But the judge won't allow Rader to control his courtroom. And Rader isn't accustomed to not being the one in charge.

Waller: Sir, let me ask you about Joseph Otero, Senior. You indicated he had torn a hole in his bag. What did you do with him then?

Rader: I put another bag over it, or either that or a-if I recollect, I think I put a-either a cloth or a t-shirt or something over it ['it' referring to Joseph Otero's head] over his head, and then a bag, another bag, then tied that down.

Waller: Did he sub-did he subsequently die?

Rader: Well, yes- I mean-I mean, I was, I didn't just stay there and watch him. I mean, he was moving around the room…

And here Rader's more sinister components are on full display. He has subdued and nearly murdered the patriarch of the family, while the remaining members of the family are bound and under his complete control as Joseph Otero fights for his life. And Mr. Otero nearly lives, but Rader, methodically, carefully, layers his suffocation material by wrapping a t-shirt or cloth over the broken bag, then places another bag on top of the cloth and then "ties him off" effectively prohibiting air to get to his lungs. But Otero is a fighter. He's bound with his hands behind his back, his feet are bound together and yet he is struggling with such force that he is able to move his body around this small room. And all during this macabre show, a show for Rader's entertainment and Joseph's family's horror, Rader is already moving to his next victim. He needs to "take out" both adults in order to lessen the threat of either being caught, or, if his captives were able to break free and Rader managed to get away, he must not leave any witnesses.

So, while Joseph is jerking and flailing around this back bedroom, Rader narrows his attention to Mrs. Julie Otero. But the room is highly charged as he approaches the bed to strangle Julie because Joseph thrashing about in his death grip and the children are both crying and screaming. He tries to work quickly, saying he "strangled Mrs. Otero and then she went out, or passed out. I thought she was dead." But she was not. Just as Joseph was losing his battle against the restraints and with his head securely covered in a bag, a piece of cloth and another bag on top for good measure, Mrs. Otero passes out from her strangulation. Rader believes she is dead and moves on to Josephina, who is lying next to her mother in the bed.

He strangles Josephina but has no intention of killing her. She is the reason he is here, and he strangles her just enough to cause her to pass out. After his quick strangulation of Josephina, he turned his attention to the only unharmed person in the room aside from the strangler himself. He leans down over nine-year-old Joseph Junior. But just as he puts the bag of Junior's head, Mrs. Otero comes to and begins to struggle against her bindings, gasping for breath. This unexpected revival causes Rader to leave Junior with the bag over his head but not yet secured so he can move back to the bed and deal with Mrs. Otero. He says she "woke back up and was pretty upset over what was going on." Rader says she begs for her son's life with such conviction that he actually removes the bag from Junior's head. But this removal was no mercy. He was simply trying to abate her fear so he could more easily murder her. He says, "So, I came back and at that point in time, strangled her for a—for the death strangle at that time." But Rader reveals that Mrs. Otero did more than beg for the life of her son. In her dying gasps she whispered, "God have mercy on your soul."

So, he strangles her again and this time, he does it right. "I went back and strangled her again," he tells the judge, "and that-that finally killed her at that time."

Rader can relax a bit now. Both Mr. and Mrs. Otero are dead. Josephina is passed out next to her dead mother's body and Junior is lying on the floor near his father's body. But Rader wasn't feeling the rush of the killings. He says that after he removed Junior's bag from his head, in compliance with Mrs. Otero's wishes, he "was really upset at that point in time." He does not reveal what upset him, but it happens after Mrs. Otero pleaded for her son's life.

It is possible she doesn't plead for her daughter's life because Josephina was passed out beside her when she came to, and she may have mistakenly believed that Josephina was already dead. But Josephina was not dead or even passed out. Her final words to her mother, just as Rader strangles her are, "I love you, Mommy."

Rader takes a quick assessment of the room to see where things stand. He sees that "Mr. Otero is down and Mrs. Otero is down." Something in this scene upset him, so after placing a bag on Junior's head, he leads him to another bedroom. He says, "I went ahead and-and took Ju—Junior, I put another bag over his head and took him to the other bedroom at this time." The judge doesn't understand why he removed Junior from the death room.

Waller: What-what did you do then?

Rader: I put a bag over his head. I put a- a cloth over his head, a t-shirt and a bag so he couldn't bite a hole in it and he subsequently died from that.

Joseph Junior' s death is now Rader's third and he adapts and applies the lessons he learned from his missteps when murdering Junior's father just moments before. So, Rader is showing himself to be clever at his craft, always prepared to improvise or adapt to unforeseen circumstances. He has long since shed his "caring" persona this late into the massacre.

Now that the boy is dead, Rader can concentrate on his main reason for stalking and then choosing this family as "his project." He wants Josephina. Rader went back into the original murder scene, the back bedroom, and Josephina was just coming around from the first strangulation. He says he leads her to the basement where he "eventually hung her." Rader is surprisingly scant on information concerning Josephina's death. The judge asks him if there is more to the hanging.

Waller: All right, you hung her in the basement?

Rader: Yes sir.

Waller: All right. Did you do anything else at that time?

Rader: Yes, I-I had some sexual fantasies. But that was after she was hung.

But in later accounts, Rader confessed that he spent some time with Josephina. He told her she would soon be joining her family, and likely this was to increase her fear because the fear, the terror, is what excited him. "Don't worry, baby," he tells her one of the times she wakes back up from his strangling, "You'll be in heaven tonight with the rest." Before he hung her, he asked her if the family had a camera—Rader liked to take pictures of himself wearing stolen women's undergarments and in various poses of bondage. So, perhaps, he wanted to use the Otero camera to take memento pictures of Josephina hanging from the basement pipe. But she told her murderer that the family didn't own a camera.

He partially disrobed her, hung her, then masturbated onto her bare legs. He would tell the judge that he, "remembers having problems with her because of her hair was in the way." He would later bring up the images of this murder in a taunting letter to the local newspaper. He wrote, "Josephina, when I hung her, really turned me on. Her pleading for mercy, then the rope took whole. She helpless. Staring at me with wide, terror filled eyes, the rope getting tighter and tighter."

After he masturbated, leaving semen on her legs and the pipe behind her, Rader begins to snoop through the house looking for items of monetary value and trophies to store in one of his hidey holes. He says he "tidied up," calling it the "right hand rule."

Rader: You go from room to room, pick everything up. I think I took Mr. Otero's watch.

Waller: Why did you take these things?

Rader: I don't know. I have no idea.

But later, when Rader was asked in a jailhouse interview why he took Joseph Otero's watch, he answered, "I didn't have one and his worked fine."

He said he walked through the house in his 'right-hand rule' procedure. He said he went from room to room and picked everything up. In his NBC interview, Rader provide more intimate information about how he was feeling after the quadruple murders.

Rader: I was really on a, not a sexual high, I was just scared high. I was really nervous, sweating, I had sweat running off me all over the place. And I just, you know, I had gloves on. I had rubber gloves, and they were just full of water, sweat. It was just really…my clothes were just soaked with sweat. Very nervous. Not like a criminal mastermind at all. This is my first that I had ever crossed that barrier.

But Rader's 'right-hand rule was not as effective as he may have thought. While he tells the police detective, he "tidied up," the Otero's older children, Charlie (15) and Carmen (13) remember the crime scene as chaotic and out of order.

Charlie: As I walked through the back door, I noticed the kitchen was in disarray. Things were on the floor. It didn't look right."

Charlie said that his sister Carmen, who entered the house before him, yelled from the back bedroom to "come quick!" When he ran down the hallway to the bedroom, he found Carmen with his parents. He said his father was "tied up and his eyes were bulging. His tongue was bit off." Police said that when they arrived, Carmen was using a pair of fingernail clippers in an attempt to cut the ties from around her mother's neck. The police took Carmen and Charlie to down to the station and the whole time the children kept telling them to "go to Josie and Joey's school." The older siblings wanted to keep the younger kids from finding their parents the way that they had. Charlie said they were at the station for "quite a while" and both the kids kept asking the police. "Did you get ahold of the little ones?" In fairness to the police officers, they had never encountered any kind of massacre to this level before.

Finally, Charlie said that the police told them, "you don't have to worry about that. They were killed also." Charlie said that when he saw his mother dead on the bed, he instantly, "lost my religion. There cannot be a God," he said. And just in case there was one, Charlie said "But if there is one, I hate him." But what he felt at the knowledge of his little siblings death trumped the emotions he felt at seeing his mother dead. He said, "When they told me about Josie and Joey, I just died inside."

Rader had very different emotions surrounding the murders. Rader was conflicted with himself because he craved attention, praise even, for his deeds, but knew he had to keep the murders a secret. To supply himself that attention, nine months after the murders, he sent a "confession letter" to the police, taking credit for the Otero murders. He wrote, "I can't stop it, so the monster goes on and hurts me as well as society." He indicated that the monster would be, "waiting in the dark, waiting, waiting, waiting." It was in this letter that he gave himself the nickname that would define him over the next thirty years. He signed the letter with this postscript:

The code words for me will be Bind them, toture, [sic] kill them. BTK., you see he at it again. They will be on the next victim.

Kathryn Doreen Bright

And it didn't take long for Rader to find his next victim. Just under three months later, on April 4, 1974, Rader entered 3217 East Thirteenth Street. This was the home of Kathryn Doreen Bright. Rader had been stalking her neighborhood, and he noticed Bright one day on a typical drive by. She was entering her front door with another person and Rader thought, "That's a possibility." In his mind he called her "that sweet kid."

Rader explained that he had many "projects" ongoing at any given time. In fact, when Judge Waller asks him to account for Bright's murder, Rader answered that he didn't "know how to exactly say that. I had many what I call 'projects.' They were different people in town that I followed, watched. Kathryn Bright was one of the next targets, I guess, as I would indicate."

Rader kept an emotional distance from the process of choosing a victim. Once his trolling produced a potential target, he would then begin stalking in earnest, taking their mail, learning their phone numbers, and even trailing them on their daily routines. But sometimes all this effort would not result in a murder. Rader nonchalantly explained this to Judge Waller.

Rader: There were many, many places in the area [I would troll]. But anyway, that's—it was just basically a selection process, worked toward it. If it didn't work, I'd just move on to something else. But in the-in the-my kind of person, stalking and trolling-you go through the trolling stage and then a stalking stage. She was in the stalking stage when this happened.

Rader broke into her house through a back door to wait for her to come home. Because he was so detailed in his stalking phase, he knew she would not be at home when he broke in and also knew that she would return shortly. He said he surveilled the house, "walking through the house and kind of figured out where I'd be if they came through." Now, Rader's use of "they" becomes controversial in that during his confession he claims that when Kathryn returned home, she was with her brother Kevin. Rader testifies that he "wasn't expecting him to be there. And come to find out, I guess they were related [Kevin was Kathryn's brother]." But this "surprise" to find Kevin in the house rings false as Rader had already confessed to stalking Kathryn and seeing her in the companionship with "another person."

He also states to Judge Waller that while he was lurking in the home, waiting for Bright to return, he walked through the house "and kind of figured out where I'd be if *they* came through [author emphasis]." He must have known and prepared for Kevin's presence there at the time of his crimes.

When the Bright siblings return to Kathryn's house, Rader ambushes them from the room "near the bedroom." He gives them the same story he offered the Otero's about being wanted in California and needing food and a car. He uses this scenario, he says, to, "kind of ease them. Make them feel better." But if Rader is looking for a hospitality award, he will soon lose his eligibility when he orders Kevin to tie up his sister. He recounts, "I think I had him tie-I think I had him tie her up first." After Kevin secures his sister's bindings, Rader then ties up Kevin. In his sentencing hearing, Waller questions Rader on the materials he carries in his "hit kit."

Waller: You indicated that you had some items to tie these people with. Did you bring these items, both to the Otero's and to this location?

Rader: The Otero's I did. I'm not really sure on the Bright's. There were some-I-when I had-In working with the police there was controversy on that. Probably, more likely I did, but if -if I had brought my own stuff and used my stuff, Kevin would probably be dead today. I'm not bragging on that. It's just a matter of fact. It's the bonds I had tau—tied him up with that he broke them, so that—

Waller: All right, sir.

Rader: It may be the same way with Kathryn. It was-it got out of hand.

By "out of hand" Rader means that the Bright siblings fought hard against him. Perhaps because the Oteros were so compliant, friendly even, at least at the beginning, he expected the Brights to fall under his command as easily. But this family was feisty, and they were not going to be "put down" without a fierce fight.

After both the Brights were bound, Rader secured his biggest threat, Kevin, to the bedposts. Rader says, "he was already secure there by the bed-tied his feet to the bedpost-one of the bedposts so he couldn't run." Because Rader had put both the Otero males on the ground and the females on the bed, it can be assumed that Kevin Bright was on the floor when Rader tied his feet to the bedpost. After he secured the male victim, he moved Kathryn, his real target, to another bedroom where he secured her. And this is where things begin to "get out of hand." Rader leaves Kathryn in the second bedroom and goes back to Kevin order to "put down" his greatest threat. But when Rader, "started strangling, the—either the garrot broke or he broke his bonds and he jumped up real quick like." This forced Rader to abandon his strangling pleasure as he pulled out one of the two guns he carried to the Bright's that day. He said he, "pulled my gun and quickly shot at him. It hit him in the head. He fell over. I could see the blood. As far as I was concerned he—you know, I thought he was down and out." Rader believed that Kevin was dead so he turned his attention back to Kathryn in the other bedroom. But here too, he found a surprise. Kathryn hadn't spent her time alone bound and compliant just patiently waiting for Rader's return. She had obviously heard Kevin fighting Rader and then heard the gunshot. She began to wrestle free from her bindings. So that when Rader, "went and started to strangle Kath-or Kathryn, she started fighting because the bonds weren't very good, and so back and forth we fought. And the struggle lasted for some time. But slowly, Rader gained the upper hand and he said he, "thought she was going down" but suddenly Rader hears Kevin moving in the other room. So, he leaves Kathryn again, thinking she "was down" and found Kevin lying on the floor injured but alive. Rader thought he might get to strangle Kevin after all but as leaned over him to do so, "he jumped up and we fought." At some point, Rader had dropped his extra gun because now Kevin had it pointed at Rader. He later would tell a journalist that, 'I just did one of those John Wayne things." Rader told the judge he had the second gun in his shoulder holster.

Waller: A should holster?

Rader: Hmm?

Waller: Did you have it in a should holster?

Rader: Yes. Mmm. I had the magnum in my shoulder holster. The other one [the one he shot Kevin Bright with] was a .22.

Rader continued to fight with Kevin, all the while worried that the magnum would go off so during the fight, Rader managed to, "jam the gun, stuck my finger in the—in there, jammed it." Rader says he didn't think to use the .22 gun in the room, because the fight was erratic. He didn't shoot Kevin with the .22 at that time. Instead, he fought to gain control over the magnum. He says he "either bit his finger or hit him or something and got away." At this point the two men are disentangled from one another and Rader uses this opportunity to grab his .22 and "shot him one more time, and I thought he was down for good that time."

So now Rader feels free to turn his attention back to Kathryn. When he approached her in the second bedroom, she was still struggling to get out of her bindings. Rader says, "at that point, I'd been fighting her. I just—and then I heard some- I don't know whether I was lose-basically losing control. The strangulation wasn't working on her." This angered Rader, who later described Kathryn's struggle saying, "she fought like a hellcat."

Rader had chosen the Brights solely so he could strangle them. But he had to shoot Kevin so that didn't work out for him, and here was Kathryn, continuing to fight against him. So he finally gives up on the idea of strangulation and decides to use the third deadly weapon he carried to this house: his knife.

Waller: You say you used the knife on her?

Rader: Yes. Yes.

Waller: What did you do with the knife?

Rader: I stabbed her. She was stab- either two or three times, either here or here, maybe two back here and one here, or maybe just two back here.

Waller: And you're-you're pointing to your lower back and your...?

Rader: Yeah, underneath the ribs.

Waller: And your lower abdomen?

Rader: Yeah. Underneath the ribs, up -up under the ribs.

Kathryn endured eleven stab wounds. The knife Rader used was part of his Boy Scout kit and almost thirty years later, at the time of Rader's arrest, that knife was still in his possession. It was found in his kitchen pantry.

Incredibly, Kathryn was not dead when Rader fled from the Brights' home on foot. When police arrived, she was able to speak with them and let them know she didn't know the person who did this to her. She would later die in the hospital.

Even with Rader believing that both Kevin and Kathryn were dead, he felt out of control of the scene. And this upset him. One of the reasons he went there was to have complete control. He told a journalist later that, "you have to control, which is the bonding. That's been a big thing with me. My sexual fantasy is of... If I'm going to kill a victim or do something to the victim is having them bound and tied. In my dreams, I had what they called 'torture chambers.' And to relive your sexual fantasies, you have to go to the kill."

Would Rader have continued killing if the Brights were his first victims, instead of the Oteros? The Oteros were his perfect victims. They were scared, compliant, and offered no resistance aside from an instinctual fight to continue breathing. Rader was in supreme control throughout the entire crime. The Brights, on the other hand, fought his authority and control from the time they were both bound until Rader left. And he didn't get to strangle anybody, which destroyed his fantasy. He said, "Well, it's a total mess. I didn't have control of it. She was bleeding; she went down."

After some time, Rader went back to check on Kevin, which is when he discovered that Kevin had escaped. Kevin later told the police that, "I played like I was dead. He left [Rader left the room]." When Kevin ran from the house, he approached, "two men across the street." One called for the police, the other took him to the hospital. Kevin Bright suffers from permanent nerve damage from the second bullet. He was so traumatized in the hospital that the police didn't tell him of his sister's murder until several days into his own healing.

Rader recalls the event with perverse excitement: "All of a sudden, the front door of the house was opened, and he was gone. I thought the police were coming at that time. I heard the door open and I thought, you know, 'that's it.' And I stepped out there, and he- I could see him running down the street. So, I quickly cleaned up everything that I could and left."

As with the Oteros, Rader attempted to steal Kathryn's vehicle, but was unable to get the keys to start her pickup. He said, "I tried, I had already had the keys to the cars and I thought I had the right key to the right car. I ran out to the car--I think it was a pickup out there. And I tried it, but it didn't work; and at that point in time, he was gone-running down the street. I thought, 'well, I'm in trouble,' so I tried it, it didn't work. So, I just took off, ran."

So, because he was convinced the police were on their way—and they were—he abandoned the idea of stealing her truck and instead legged it the five blocks to the Wichita State University campus where his own car was parked. He made a clean getaway. Rader would not kill again for nearly three more years.

But his monstrous ego needed fed. Several months after he nearly killed Kevin and successfully killed Kathryn, Rader was experiencing a letdown. The adrenaline from the murders was gone and he was unable to fulfill his fantasies because he was not able to successfully strangle either one of them.

It was in October of 1974, six months after Kathryn's murder, that the police arrested someone for the Otero murders. This incensed Rader—he hated the idea of someone else getting credit for his crimes. To get some attention back on himself, he called the Wichita Eagle and told a reporter about a hidden letter in an engineering book at the Wichita Library. The reporter did not scoop the story as Rader had hoped, but rather called the police who did find the letter tucked inside the book.

The letter, riddled with Rader's spelling and grammatical errors, boasted of the Otero crimes in such a way as to prove that he was the murderer. He needed recognition for the work and wrote, "I did it myself with noone's help." It was in this letter that he provided the police and press with his chosen nickname of "BTK." This letter would be the first of 19 he would send to the police and the press, seeking attention and respect for his crimes. His final letter would be the one that led police to his church, and then his to his office, and then, finally, to him.

SHIRLEY VIAN RELFORD

After Rader wrote his first letter, taking both pride and responsibility for the Otero murders, he went dark for nearly three years. But in March 1977, Rader moved past his trolling stage and began to stalk a Cheryl Greene that he claims he met in a bar. On March 17, 1977, Rader was intent on making her his next victim. But fortunately for her, she was not home when he approached her house. However, her absence would prove to be the worst thing in the world for Shirley Vian.

Waller: Now let's turn to count six. In that count they claim on March 17, 1977…that you unlawfully killed Shirley Vian, maliciously, willfully, deliberately and with premeditation….Can you tell me what you did on that day?

Rader tells the judge that finding Vian was "completely random." He had been stalking another potential victim [Cheryl Greene] who lived across from the Dillard's department store. This Dillard's is the same store that he drove the stolen Otero car to and threw their car keys on top of the Dillard's roof.

So, he parked at the Dillard's and walked over to the "Project Greene" house and brazenly knocked on the front door. But no one answered. Rader claims he "was all keyed up" by that time, so he started walking through the neighborhood scanning for a potential victim. He had his hit kit with him, and he was in the mood. He told Judge Waller that he,

"...just started going through the neighborhood. I had been through the neighborhood before. I kind of knew a little-little of the layout of the neighborhood. I knew the back alleys, knew where some, certain people lived."

Rader said that when he got to Hydraulic Street, he ran into a five-year-old boy named Steve Relford. It is probable that Rader knew which house—and mother—the boy belonged to, as this area was a habitual trolling ground for him. He asked the boy to look at a picture to offer an ID. He said he used the picture as a ruse—the picture was of his own wife and son. The boy, obviously, didn't recognize Rader's own family in the photo and continued to his home.

Rader began to walk to a different house, but all the while, was watching to see which house the boy entered. Rader knocked on the house he walked to, but there was no answer. He then walked directly to the house he had watched the boy enter. Rader knocked on the door and Steve, a child, answers, with two younger children (6 and 4) behind him.

Rader says he "showed 'em a picture and asked 'em if they could ID the picture, and, at that time I, I had the gun here and I just kind of forced myself in. You know, just opened the door and walked in and then pulled the pistol." This .357 magnum was the very gun that Kevin Bright had wrestled from Rader during their struggle inside Kathryn's home. Rader said that once he gained entry, he turned off the tv and closed all the blinds. The strange sounds alerted the children's mother who came out from her bedroom in a dressing gown. She was home sick that day.

She was startled to see Rader standing in her living room with a gun. He told her he "had a problem with sexual fantasies" and while she processed that information, shocked and afraid, looking at her three young children, he added that he, "might have to tie her up and that-and I might have to tie the kids up. He pointed the gun toward the children to enforce her compliance.

He began tying up the children, but they were crying loudly, and he thought, "oh, this is not going to work." So, he then solicited his target's help in forcing the children into the bathroom. He says before he tied the door shut, "we put some toys and blankets and odds and ends there for the kids, make them as comfortable as we could." Rader's use of the plural pronoun "we" is notable in that he seems to believe that he and Shirley were in this together.

His belief that she existed solely to satisfy him fits into the narcissistic diagnosis he will receive in prison. He doesn't view Shirley as an independent, autonomous human with her own free will. When he says, "we did this for the children and we then did that," he is combining their purposes. In fact, of course, Shirley's purpose was to keep her children alive while Rader's purpose was to keep her children controlled until he could kill them.

Rader explores this idea as well when he said, "I don't think it was actually the person that I was after; I think it was the dream. I know that's not really nice to say about a person, but they were basically an object. That's all they were. I had more satisfaction building up to it and afterwards than I did the actual killing of the person."

The bathroom appeared to be a Jack and Jill style, meaning it connected two bedrooms together. So, he tied one door closed but had Shirley help him, "shove—she went back and helped me shove the bed up against the other bathroom door." After he had secured the children, he sat with Shirley and they both smoked a cigarette. He said she was "very nervous." He then tied Shirley up, but either because of her illness, or, perhaps more relevant, her fear, she threw up.

Ever the gentle murderer, Rader claims he went to the kitchen to get her a glass of water and "comforted her a little." In court, Rader skips the part where he stripped, her but even while doing so, he assured Shirley that he was not going to rape her, that his fantasy only involves tying her up.

He doesn't add, of course, that the ultimate fulfillment of his fantasy is to strangle her to death.

He bound her legs together using a long rope and black electrical tape. Though Rader did not rape his victims, his crimes were undoubtedly sexually motivated. Rader stripped her naked, tied her up then would masturbate on her legs after he strangled her. This is a sexual assault.

The children were crying this entire time and, to add to their horror, they could see what was happening to their mother through a crack in the door. When they were securing the children into the bathroom, Shirley told Rader that she expected her neighbor to come over since she had been sick. So, Rader had this time pressure in the back of his mind, which eroded his sense of control. Added to that tension was the sound of the children screaming and crying in the bathroom during his fetishized binding of Shirley.

When the judge asked Rader how he strangled her, he said that after he got her the glass of water, he "went ahead and tied her up and then put a bag over her head and strangled her." The judge asked if the bag was plastic and Rader answered that, "Yes sir, I think it was, but I could be wrong on that." But then seconds later says, "It was something-I'm sure it was a plastic bag, yeah." But Rader would have to secure the bag and so the judge asked for more details.

Rader: I actually-I think on that one [note his detachment from seeing Shirley as a human by his use of a non-human pronoun 'that'] that I had tied-tied her legs to the bedposts and worked up with the rope all the way up, and then, what I had left over, I looped over her neck.

Waller: All right, so you used this rope to strangle her?

Rader: Yes, uh-huh. I think- I think it was that I tied her body with. Mm-hmm.

Rader's plan was to then strangle each of the three crying children, but Shirley unwittingly saved their lives when she told Rader that a neighbor would be stopping over to check on the family. Rader says her children "were really banging on the door, hollering and screaming, and then the telephone rang, and they had talked about earlier a neighbor's gonna check on 'em so I cleaned everything up real quick-like, and got out of there."

Rader left the children trapped in the bathroom staring at their naked, dead mother lying on the bed. He calmly walked back through the neighborhood, over to the Dillard's parking lot and slowly drove away. The judge asked him to back up. He wanted details of Rader's clean-up efforts.

Waller: Now when you say you cleaned everything…

Rader: Well, I mean I put my stuff-I had a briefcase. Whatever I have laying around [the crime scene], ropes, tape cords, I threw that in there, my-you know, whatever, you know, that I had brought to the house.

Waller: Had you brought that to the Bright residence also or—

Rader: Yeah, there is some-there-I-I think there's some basic stuff, but I don't remember bringing total stuff like I did to some of the others.

Waller: Was this a kit you prepared

Rader: Yeah, I…

Waller: Beforehand?

Rader: Yes, I call it my hit kit.

Years later, Steve Relford, now an adult, remembers the invasion—much

differently than Rader. For example, Relford says that when he told Rader he was going to untie the rope that held the bathroom door closed, Rader shouted, "You better not…I'll blow your [expletive] head off!" Relford confirmed that he and his younger siblings could hear and see everything the BTK was doing to their mother.

He says, "I remember seeing my mama being stripped, her hands behind her back, plastic bag over her head, rope tied around her neck." He says he feels guilty because he was the one who opened the door to this monster. "I let the BTK into my house." He says he remembers remaining trapped in the bathroom almost forty minutes after his mother's murder. His younger brother broke out through the bathroom window but Steve and his youngest sibling couldn't get out that way. Eventually, Steve managed to break the bathroom door but by then, his mother was already dead and Dennis Rader had made a very clean escape.

He adds that, "it's been 28 years, and I hope to hell I meet this [expletive] face to face."

NANCY FOX

Rader took nine months off after killing Shirley Bright before he broke into 843 South Pershing Street to strangle 25-year-old Nancy Jo Fox. Rader claimed he considered Nancy Jo as a potential project well before his attack. He said that on one of his trolling expeditions, he "noticed her going into the house one night. I put her down as a potential victim." When in court, the judge asks Rader to explain his "trolling" or "stalking." Rader is very proud of his work as a serial killer and obliges Waller.

Rader: "Well, I don't know if you read much about serial killers, they go through what they call different phases. That's one of the phases they go through is a trolling stage. You lay—basically you're looking for a victim at that time and that can either be trolling for months or years. But once you lock in on a certain person then you become stalking, and that might be several of them, but you really hone in on that person. They basically come-that's-that's the victim, or at least, that's what you want them to be."

Once Rader graduated Fox from a simple trolling exercise to an actual project or victim, he began to stalk in earnest. He called her "Project Fox Hunt." He said that, "at first she was spotted, [note the predator/prey terminology] and then I did a little homework." By 'homework' Rader means that he began to become familiar with her routine. This included raiding her mailbox to determine her name and following her to work to find out where she was employed. She worked at Helzberg Jewelry Store in the Wichita Mall. Rader, ever coy, always on the prowl, actually visited her at work on several occasions. Her job at Helzberg was a part-time gig for Nancy. She only worked there two nights a week and occasionally on Saturdays. Her fulltime job was for The Law Company, a construction business, as their fulltime secretary.

Her coworker, Cindy Duckett remembers Nancy Fox as a hard worker who "smiled a lot, she joked a lot." Duckett said that Fox was "more mature than the rest of the girls." Nancy's sister, Beverly Fox agreed: "She was outgoing, very friendly. She was one to speak her mind. She didn't keep quiet."

On a cold December night in 1977, with Shirley Vian Relford buried less than a year, Rader approached Nancy Fox's house on South Pershing Street. He says of that night, "I just selected a night, which was this particular night, to try it, and it worked out." And indeed, it worked out for Rader, but not for Nancy Fox.

He tells the court that he parked his car a few blocks away, which was his routine by now, six victims in. And, like he did in the Relford's neighborhood, he casually walked to Nancy's house and knocked on the front door. Now, he knew she wasn't home because he had spent months tracking and stalking her. He said he knocked "at the door, first, to make sure, see if anybody was in there, 'cause I knew she arrived home at a particular time from where she worked."

So Rader was feeling confident when he knocked on the door. It's possible he felt a sense of bravado ownership in knocking on the front doors of his victims. It's a brazen thing to do, and many of his victims died during daylight hours, meaning any one of the neighbors could see or later identify him. But luck was with the wicked in that he was never identified this way. Once he knocked on the door, and receiving the unsurprising no answer, he slipped to the back of the apartment to cut the phone line. He cased the other apartments, looking for a witness, and when he found none, he "broke in and waited for her to come home." Like his other victim's houses, Rader walked through the house while waiting. He said he ended up in the kitchen.

When Fox arrived home at her scheduled time, she found Rader in the kitchen where he told her his tired tale of: "I had a problem, a sexual problem, that I would have to tie her up and have sex with her." Again, Rader's language is astonishing. He believes that his "problem" garners him the right to violate Nancy Fox as a solution. He speaks as if she owes him this solution to his "problem."

In court he said that "she was a little upset." So, "we talked for a while. She smoked a cigarette. While we smoked a cigarette I went through her purse, identifying some stuff." Nancy Fox was the second victim Rader shared a cigarette with; Shirley Vian was the first. He is playing the role of cat to the victims' mouse.

While they share the intimacy of the cigarette, with Fox clearly panicked, Rader calmly dumps out her purse on the kitchen table as if he already owns everything that is hers. He said that as he rooted through her handbag, he was "identifying stuff." By the time the cigarette was finished, Nancy exerted the only control she had in this situation. She stood up and said, "let's get this over with so I can call the police." Rader also stood when Nancy asked if she could use the bathroom. He allowed her this dignity but told her "when she came out to make sure she was undressed." Fox complied and when she exited the bathroom naked, he handcuffed her. This was a new procedure for Rader and the judge wants some clarification.

Waller: You handcuffed her?

Rader: Sir?

Waller: You handcuffed her. You had a pair of handcuffs?

Rader: Yes, sir. Uh-huh. Mmm-hmm.

Waller: What happened then?

Rader: Well…I handcuffed her and lay her on the bed.

From here, Rader seems confused about the timing of tying her feet. At first, he says he tied her feet but that he was "partially undressed to a certain degree." He says he "got on top of her" but here he fumbles for the memory. Or pretends to for affect. He tells the judge that he "reached over—took either-either her feet were tied or not tied but anyway, I took-I think I had a belt. I took the belt and strangled her with it at that time."

Because the act of strangulation is Rader's sexual impetus, he then takes the belt off her and replaces the belt with a pair of pantyhose. The pantyhose seem important to Rader; they somehow hold meaning to him as he speculated in open court that he "can't remember the colors right now." By this he meant the various shades of pantyhose that are available, for example, nude, charcoal, or suntan.

So, he removes the belt, and this partially revives her as he shuffles about to replace the belt with the pantyhose. As he is rearranging his murder weapons, he whispers to her, "in her ear a little bit. I told her I was the BTK, I was a bad guy. And then she really squirmed and then– I pulled-put the pressure down on it."

Again, he subjugates her to a pronoun reserved for objects: 'it'. But remember that, to Rader, the person doesn't actually matter. He sees each victim as an object. So, unto this end, it likely makes little difference if the object is alive or dead. Yes, he derives his sexual pleasure during the actual strangulation event, but many times he either masturbates again, after his victim is dead, or only masturbates after his victim is dead. Rader feels it's important to inform the judge that he did not 'rape' this victim despite the fact that his attack was motivated by his sexual predilections.

Waller: All right, you had sexual relations with her…

Rader: No.

Waller: …before?

Rader: No. No. I told her I was, but I did not.

It's possible that Rader tells his victims that he intends to rape them to add to their terror. The more afraid they are, the more in control he is and the more he feeds his sexual ego. Rader didn't sexually penetrate any of his victims, but every attack was sexual in nature. And for a woman to be disrobed, tied up, terrorized, strangled and masturbated over, this is a violent sexual attack.

Once Rader masturbated on Fox's exposed legs, after strangling her to death, he gets off the bed and dresses himself. He then does his "right hand rule" by sweeping the house both to pick up any item he may have dropped from his hit kit, but also to steal any mementos to use as trophies and as evidence to taunt the police. Like many of his victims, Rader stole Nancy's driver's license that he had found while poking through her purse at the abduction stage of the murder. It's notable to recall her sister, Cindy Duckett's, observation that her sister was the type of girl who "spoke her mind." She did not keep quiet. Perhaps, when Nancy Fox, sitting across from her soon to be murderer stood up and said, "let's get this over with so I can call the police" it was her way of not only controlling the situation to the limited amount available to her, but also to threaten Rader, perhaps scare him a bit by letting him know that while he may rape her, she will have the final word. It was bold of her to make such a proclamation at such a time. It shows courage and pluck.

When Rader walked the few blocks down to his car, just after sexually assaulting and murdering Nancy Fox, he would cool off for nine years before stalking and killing again. Nancy Fox's driver's license would not reappear from the bowels of Rader's hidey hole until 2004 when he would send it to the police along with a doll whose feet and hands were bound and head was covered with a plastic bag. He would later tell police that, because this particular sexual assault and murder was completed without any interruptions or unexpected circumstances, he referred to it as his "perfect hit."

But just as he grew impatient after killing Kathryn Bright, wanting attention and seeking accolades when he called the reporter at the Wichita, Rader grew bored and discontent in his cooling off period after Nancy Fox's murder. First of all, he wasn't reading about it in any papers and didn't hear about it on the news. And this agitated him. He wanted the world to see what a clever killer he was. So, he made a rather bold move. He drove to a local phone booth—this was before cell phones and phone booths were found on street corners and outside shops and convenient stores. He dialed 911 and told the dispatcher that, "yes, you will find a homicide at 843 Pershing. Nancy Fox." The call, of course, was recorded, but the dispatcher interrupts Rader by trying to get him to repeat the address.

Operator 1: Dispatcher

Rader: Yes. You will find a homicide at 843 South Pershing. Nancy Fox

Operator 1: I'm sorry sir, I can't understand you. What is the address?

Operator 2: I believe 843 South Pershing…

Rader: That is correct.

In a thirty-one second call, and speaking just fifteen words, he let the police know of his murder. He said later that Nancy Fox was his favorite victim. He said of her: "Although she gave me a lot of verbal static, she cooperated; she didn't fight me." He went on to proudly discuss his seventh victim in terms of how well he executed her assault and murder: "I had complete control of her, that's why it was one of the more, more enjoyable kills, as I call them." Much later, after his court testimony, it was reported that he was sexually aroused by the discussion of Fox's death. He was reported as saying, with much satisfaction, "Fox went the way I wanted it."

A month after his call to 911, he would write a poem about her, one entitled *Oh! Death to Nancy* and send it to the Wichita Police. The phone call itself was traced to the phone booth, but, of course, Rader was long gone. Additionally, the quality of the recording was so poor that it wasn't released to the public until 1979 and even then, despite it being listened to by people close to him, no one was able to identify Dennis Rader as the caller.

Rader was not idle during this cooling off phase. On February 10th, 1978, just one month after he sent his poem to the police, Rader sent a letter to KAKE-TV claiming responsibility for killing Shirley Vian and Nancy Fox. He also admitted to a third, unnamed victim. It was after this publicity stunt that the Chief Investigator, Richard LaMunyon, announced to the public that Wichita was home to a serial killer. He cautioned the public to remain aware as he was certain the predator would kill again.

And Rader almost did kill again. In April (one of his favorite months to strike), Rader had stalked a 63-year-old woman. But his murder did not go as flawlessly as his experience with Nancy Fox. On April 28, 1979, Rader broke into Anna Williams's home, but she returned later than his stalking phase had led him to believe. Williams had been to a square dance and afterward, dropped in unplanned to visit her daughter. Rader, who was sitting in her dark kitchen drinking water, soon becomes frustrated and then angry. He took one of her scarves and left a note saying, "Be glad you weren't here. Because I was." It was becoming too late for Rader to wait any longer. But he didn't leave without attempting to continue to terrorize the woman. He later mailed her a poem telling her he was in her home. He titled the poem, *Oh Anna, Why Didn't you Appear?* In the poem, Rader writes that, "T'was the perfect plan of deviant pleasure so bold on that Spring nite." Rader confessed to a prison psychologist that Anna wasn't the only one to get away. He claimed, "There's a lot of lucky people out there…didn't make it to their house…or for some reason, I didn't go. There's lots of lucky people out there, yes."

On August 15, 1979, just four months after Rader narrowly missed killing Anna Williams, the police decided to make Rader's phone recording to the 911 dispatch regarding Nancy Fox's murder available to the public. The media, already intensely involved in the BTK stories, played the recording over and over. Radio and television stations played the recording which provides police with more than 100 tips. But they were unable to connect the tips to Rader and so he remains free to kill again.

MARINE HEDGE

After his long hiatus—almost nine years—Rader was ready to strike again. On April 27, 1985, Rader set his sights closer to home. Just six doors down from his own family home, he began to stalk his neighbor, Marine Hedge, who, at 53 years old, was thirteen years older than her murderer. Rader said that it was easier to stalk her as she lived within sight of his home. He named her "The Cookie Project." Hedge worked as a shift supervisor at the Medical Center Coffee Shop. She lost her husband a year before her own murder, which would tragically leave her four children orphaned.

Waller: Can you tell me what occurred on that day?

Rader: Well, actually, kind of like the others. She was chosen. I went through the different phases, stalking phase, and since she lived down the street from me, I could watch the coming and going quite easily. On that particular date, I -I had a-another commitment.

Rader's testimony became a very confusing tangle of circumstances and events that seemed to break from his previous patterns. When, in the past, he walked boldly up to the front door and knocked, or snuck around back and cut the phone line and broke in, the Hedge murder seems to be an elaborate plan intent on misdirection. It's as if Rader was playing the role of a spy for an audience of one: himself.

After Rader completed his "previous commitment," instead of driving home and parking in his driveway and simply walking the six doors down to his neighbor's house, he parked "over at Woodlawn and 21st Street at a bowling alley there at that time." He brought along a pair of clothes to change into; perhaps his previous commitment required him to wear clothes that would be unsuitable for a murder. But he changed clothes, and it's unclear if he went into the bowling alley to change or if he changed in his car in the parking lot. But he does eventually enter the bowling alley. He says, "I went to the bowling alley, went in there under the pretense of bowling." But instead of bowling, he called a taxi.

If he was attempting to produce an alibi—something he didn't bother with any of his seven previous victims—he did so poorly. He said that immediately upon entering the bowling alley, he called for a taxi. When the taxi arrived, Rader got in carrying his "hit kit" inside his bowling bag. For some reason, Rader wanted the taxicab driver to think he was drunk, so he "took some beer, I just took some beer and washed it around my mouth, and the guy could probably smell alcohol on me."

Why he needed this fake taxi drive from the bowling alley back to the neighborhood both he and Marine Hedge lived in remains a mystery. He took a good deal of time creating this elaborate scenario for no one in particular. He told the driver, "to let me out so I could get some fresh air…" at which time, the disinterested cabby dropped him off in Rader's own neighborhood. In his court testimony, Rader relived the scheme for the judge who seemed confused by all the unnecessary subterfuge.

Waller: All right, where does she live?

Rader: 62-what is it-42-54. 6254? [he asks the judge then answers his own question] 6254.

Waller: All right, what was the…

Rader: North Independence.

Waller: All right. When you walked over there, what happened next.

In this exchange, Waller seems intent on trying to fit Rader's long, sloppy, convoluted plan to make sense within the context of the murder. Which, of course, it does not. Parking in a bowling alley, changing clothes, swishing beer in his mouth, the superfluous ride in the taxi, none of it makes sense when attempting to understand Hedge's murder.

Here, perhaps Dr. Ramsland can make some sense of his actions before this, his eighth, murder. She says, "his narcissistic personality led him to imagine himself as kind of a spy." She writes that his spy-like character "contributed to both his need for secrecy and layers." She argues that this deception, like attempting to make a taxicab driver believe he was drunk, increases "his sense of invulnerability" which would, of course, eventually lead to his capture.

When Rader approached her house after this circuitous trip around town, he discovered her car, a 1976 Monte Carlo, is in the driveway, and this interrupted his plan: "I was going to have sexual fantasies" [while walking to her house]. But her car in driveway startled him. He told Judge Waller that "lo and behold, her car was there. And I thought, 'gee, she's not supposed to be home.'" And here again one sees the enormousness of Rader's ego. How dare Marine Hedge commit an act of free will outside of Rader's intentions? But Rader, who was, "keyed up" was not going to let this little disturbance in his plan cause him to abandon all he had worked so hard for.

He said he, "very carefully snuck into the house, kind of like a cat burglar, and after checking the house, she wasn't there. So, Rader rested back into his comfort zone. He trolled through the house to wait for her. But he didn't wait long. He said that shortly after he entered her home, he heard, "the doors rattle, so I went—went back to one of the bedrooms." And here Rader committed a horrifying act, the type that causes millions of women to check under their beds and behind the shower curtains. He hid in the back of the house while she entertained a male visitor who brought her home. Rader said the visitor stayed for, "an hour or so," and then left.

Hedge, who believed herself to be alone, undresses, performed her ablutions—all the while with Rader listening and tracking her very private movements—and then put herself to bed. Rader said he, "waited until the wee hours of the morning. I then proceeded to sneak into her bedroom and flip the lights on real quick like. I just-I didn't want her to flip her lights on." In other words, he wanted to terrify her. He succeeded. He says, "she screamed, and I jumped on the bed and strangled her manually." In some interviews, Rader uses the term "throttled" to describe his method. During his testimony, Judge Waller seems more interested in Rader's relationship with Hedge than with the murder itself.

Waller: All right, now were you wearing any kind of a disguise or mask at this time?

Rader: No. No.

Waller: You indicated this woman lived down the street from you. Did she know you?

Rader: Casually. We'd walk by and wave. She—She liked to work in her yard as well as I liked to work, and it's just a neighborly type of thing. It wasn't anything personal, I mean, just a neighbor.

Judge Waller then turned his attention back to the murder. He asked Rader why he turned on the bathroom lights before he killed her. Rader explained that he did so, "just to- so I could get some light in there." In other words, so he could fan his sexual flame with her terror. If he couldn't see the look of surprise and fear in her eyes, the sexual component would not be as strong. And it seemed to work. Rader went on to say that after he manually strangled her to death, and since he was "in the sexual fantasy" that he, "went ahead and stripped her and probably went ahead and –I'm not for sure if I tied her up at that point in time, but anyway, she was nude, and I put on a blanket, went through her purse, some personal items in the house, figured out how I was going to get her out of there."

And here, Rader broke from his tradition of fleeing the house, leaving the bodies behind to be found by loved ones. Rader's fantasy concerning Project Cookie was well developed. His ultimate goal was to kill her so he could pose her at the church. He confessed, "Alive or dead, she was going to that church."

He had created this whole unique scenario surrounding Hedge's murder. It could be that he had ample time to play and expand on his fantasies. With the other murders, many of which occurred during the day, he had to account for his time both to his boss and his family. On this occasion, he was away as a Scout Leader for his son's boy scout sleep away. He would say of that night, "It's a good cover for a guy like me to go camp out and slip away." So, he had all night to play. He only had to make it back to the campsite by breakfast. He used this time well.

As in previous murders, Rader used the victim's car but, in this case, he didn't use it as a means of getting away from the crime scene. This time, he took the crime scene with him. Rader placed Hedge's naked body onto a blanket and dragged her out to the car where he then moved his victim's body to the trunk. This treatment of her body was especially cruel considering that, at her memorial, many people would comment that she was "always well dressed."

He wanted to transport her to a second location. And he knew exactly what would give him the most sexual satisfaction while, at the same time, play big for the cameras. He "took her over to Christ Lutheran Church." Rader would have had the keys to the church as he served as the Congregant President. He said he took her to the older section, "and took some pictures of her." Judge Waller inquired about the pictures in the same prurient way the press does once he is finally caught.

On the night of her murder, Rader dragged her naked body into the church vestry, and he poses her in different forms of bondage under the rack wear the choir robes are stored. He then drags her to the alter where he continued to take polaroid pictures of her in various bondage poses. He said, "She was already dead, so I took pictures of her in different forms of bondage. So anyway—that's probably the— the main thing. But, anyway, after that I moved her back out to the car and then we went east on 53rd. And here again, Rader conscribes his victim to become complicit when he says "we went east on 53rd" as if Hedge was his amiable companion, instead of lying naked and dead in the trunk of her own car.

Rader drove around for a good while, "trying to find a place to hide her, hide her body," when he settles on "a ditch, a low place on the north side of the road and hid her there."

Waller: All right. You say you 'hid her there,' did you…

Rader: Well, there were some trees, some brush and I laid that overtop of her body.

The next day her handbag was found, but without any ID, as Rader collected IDs from all his victims as trophies. Hedge's car was discovered four days later with her blanket and bedspread in the trunk. And then, just under a week from her murder, police found her naked body in a ditch about seven miles from their neighborhood. Although she was found with knotted pantyhose near her body, the coroner determined her cause of death to be manual strangulation. This type of repeated strangulation, allowing the victim to "come back" and then strangling them again, was not discussed during his sentencing testimony.

But Rader certainly earned his "T" for torture in the BTK name, because he often strangled his victims multiple times and with various devices—his hands, a garret, pantyhose and rope. Rader's sexual motivation lay in his control over the victim as they died. So as often as he could have each victim "die" would increase his sexual pleasure. Marine Hedge, "a petite, charming woman" had spent her last night alive playing bingo with her boyfriend.

VICKI WEGERLE

Rader would commit no known crimes for almost eighteen months before he set his stalking eyes on 28-year-old Vicki Wegerle. Wegerle lived in one of Rader's trolling neighborhoods at 2404 West 13th Street. She caught his attention when he heard her playing the piano during one of his reconnaissance missions. Rader quickly moved Wegerle from the "possibility" list to an actual target. He called her his "Project Piano," or, as a shorthand, "Project P."

Rader: Vicki was—Wegerle was another potential victim. I went through those different phases, locked in on her, as I would call it, and decided that I would try that date [September 16, 1986].

Rader, feeling impervious to capture by this point, drove his own personal car to her street. He disguised himself as a telephone repair person but wore what was essential his "hit clothes."

Rader: Hit clothes. Basically different, you know, things that I need to get rid of later, not-not the same kinds of clothes that I had on. I-I don't what other better word use. Crime clothes or hit clothes. I just call them hit clothes.

He told the judge that he went to Wegerle's house on his lunch break but he arrived to her door just after ten a.m. As with his unnecessary ruse involving gargling with beer to make a taxicab driver think he was drunk, Rader put on a telephone repair helmet and carried a briefcase. But he didn't go directly to her door. He first "went to another address just to kind of size up the house." He said he had "walked by it a couple of times, but I wanted to check it a little bit more." Rader actually knocked on the neighbor's door to inform her that the repair men were working in the area. But all the while, he kept his sites on the Wegerle house.

With his casing of her house complete, Rader approached her front door. He knew she was home because, "I could hear a piano sound." When she answered, he "asked her if I could come check her telephone lines inside." He played his little spy game a bit longer, claiming he "went over and found where the telephone was, simulated that I was checking the telephone." To secure his façade, he said, "I had a make-believe instrument." When Vicki looked away, Rader pulled out his trusty pistol and "asked her if she'd go back to the bedroom with me."

Here again, Rader displays a complete disconnect from the situation. He had unlawfully entered her home, held her at gunpoint and then "asked her if she'd go back to the bedroom with me" as if he was asking her to prom. This myopic view guides Rader in all that he does. Many of the answers he offered the judge about specifics during each murder show this one-sided viewpoint. He sometimes even makes the victims complicit, acting as if they are a partnership. The victim herself is meaningless to Rader outside of that person's role in fulfilling his sexual fantasies. He has no consideration for any humans, not just women but men and children as well. They are either compliant or he kills them. And then when he's finished with the compliant ones, he kills them as well.

Vicki Wegerle was not compliant. Rader managed to get her back to the bedroom but once there, she struggled to escape his attempts to tie her up. He said, "I used some material that was in- I'm not sure but I-I think I used some material that they had in their bedroom." During this struggle for control, Wegerle is at a disadvantage for two reasons: one, Rader holds the weapon and, two, her two-year-old son, Brandon, is sitting in the living room playing with toys.

In fact, when Rader first pulled the gun, Vicki became hysterical, "How about my kid?" she cried. Rader answered, "I don't know about your kid." So, Wegerle, unsure of Rader's capabilities, must have considered a longer game type strategy. If she is able to get away from his grip, will she be able to grab her son and run to safety? But Wegerle had one advantage that Rader knows nothing about. She knows her husband, Bill is on his way home for his lunch break. She knew if she could hold out long enough, fight hard enough, she could yet escape Rader's plans for her. And so, she began the fight of her life. Rader would later say that "she fought harder than any of my other victims." Once Rader did manage to restrain her with the hastily-grabbed fabric, he attempted to strangle her, but she broke free of her bindings and began scratching at his face and neck. He said she was "hysterical." Rader was pushed into a circumstance he disliked. Rader says that, "after I tied her hands, she broke that, and we started fighting, and we fought quite a bit back and forth. The judge seemed interested in this battle for her life.

Waller: All right, she was physically fighting you?

Rader: Oh yeah. Yes, sir. Mm-hmm.

Waller: What happened then?

Rader: Finally got the hand on her and got a-a nylon sock and started strangling her.

Waller: So you wrapped a stocking around her neck?

Rader: Yes. Mm-hmm. I finally gained-gained on her and-and-put her down and I thought she was dead, but apparently, she wasn't.

So even in the throes of death, Vicki kept fighting. But as much as she fought, Rader fought harder. He finally managed to kill her, or anyway, suffocate her enough to appear dead.

Rader: ...after she was down and not moving anymore, I-I-I rearranged her clothes a little bit and took some quick photos---I think three of them-if I remember-and there was a lot of commotion.

Wegerle had informed Rader during their struggle that her husband was on his way, so he did not have the luxury of time that he experienced in most of his other crime scenes. The only other hurried, chaotic crime scene out of all nine was Kathryn Bright's murder because her brother, Kevin, had escaped. So, Rader, knowing Vicki's husband was expected home for lunch, made quick work of his clean-up process.

Rader: So, I had to get out of there pretty quick. The dogs were raising a lot of Cain in the back, the doors, the windows were all open in the house, a lot of noise when we were fighting, so I left pretty quickly after that. Put everything in the briefcase and had her-I had already gone through her purse, got the keys to her car and used her car for my getaway.

When Rader fled the scene, Vicki's husband, Bill passed him very close to the house. Bill Wegerle said, "I saw my own car going the opposite direction of the house but couldn't identify the driver." As Rader drove away in safety and anonymity, Bill ran into the house and found their little boy, Brandon, unharmed still sitting in the living room. Bill rushed through the house calling for Vickie. He found her in the master bedroom lying on the floor behind their bed.

She was still alive.

She went on to survive the trip to the hospital, but her injuries were too severe to save her. She never regained consciousness and was pronounced dead several hours later. Unfortunately for her husband Bill, the BTK killer was not a suspect. Rader had been in such a long cooling off period that he was currently beneath the authority's notice. This, of course, brought Rader out to play once more, but not until Bill Wegerle suffered through the police, and then the community's suspicions.

The police suspected Bill, and he was subjected to two polygraph tests. He was so stressed and distraught over the loss of his beloved wife that he failed both tests. This was a nightmare for Bill, because failing those tests meant the police only pursued one suspect: Bill Wegerle. And then his community turned against him. His daughter, Stephanie, recalls one of her middle school teachers telling her own son that, "me and my dad were bad people and to stay away from us."

Twenty years later, Bill Wegerle would sue Rader for the wrongful death of his wife, Vicki. At Rader's sentencing Bill addressed him saying, "The past couple of days, the court, the news media and the general public knows what kind of person he is. The vicious, cruel individual he is. It's all in the light now. There's no punishment that you can exact upon him that will satisfy our needs."

Rader later reported to be "disappointed" in the Wegerle murder. For one thing, he was hurried and harried by the dog's barking and the pressure of the impending arrival of Vicki's husband. These combined factors prohibited him from experiencing the sexual release that he drove him to commit the murder in the first place. And, for another reason—she was still alive when he left the house.

As the police continued to publicly proclaim Bill as a person of interest, Rader became angry. It scratched at him that the BTK wasn't getting any credit. But he continued to creep in the shadow of anonymity for just over four years. On January 19, 1991, Rader would murder his final victim. Rader would not know it would be his final victim in that he planned to kill once more after this murder as a "retirement kill." But his own hubris would stop him after his tenth victim.

DOLORES DAVIS

olores Davis (Dee) was a 62-year-old woman who lived on her own. Perhaps remembering the vicious fight Vicki Wegerle put up against him, Rader began targeting older women who would be weaker and less able to interfere with his fantasy of control and dominion. Davis, a divorcee with two grown children and a couple of grandchildren, was retired from her job as a secretary of a fuel company. She had worked for them for twenty-five years, exemplifying some of her attributes including dedication, devotion and loyalty. Bored in her retirement, Davis began selling Mary Kay cosmetics to stay active in the community. Additionally, she became a fierce advocate for animal right's issues.

Her home at 6226 North Hillside Street was situated close to a dog kennel which is why Rader called her "Project Dogside." As with the Marine Hedge murder, Rader used his getaway as a Boy Scout Leader to his son's troop's camping weekend as his alibi, should he ever be questioned (he wasn't). But the Boy Scout camping weekend would provide him with ample time to enjoy and savor his murder. Rader was still stinging from the interrupted and rushed murder of Vicki Wegerle just over three years before. That murder was his most disappointing and he intended to avoid the pitfalls he experienced there. It's interesting to note that both times Rader left the Scout Camp to commit murder he obfuscates in court about his exact activity by failing to mention the name "Boy Scouts."

Rader: That particular day, I had some commitments.

Rader used this same term "commitments" when confessing to Marine Hedge's murder. He told the judge,

Rader: On that particular date I-I had a- another commitment. I came back from that commitment…

In both cases, he refuses to place himself at the Boy Scout Camp. Perhaps he is attempting to protect his son, who attended both Boy Scout camps as a scout camper. But more likely, Rader was protecting the Boy Scout association itself as he was a very proud and very active member of their leadership team.

On this particular night in January, the 19th, 1991, Rader slipped away from camp and drove his car near his home and the Baptist Church. He had access to the church because of his Scout duties, and let himself in to change into his hit clothes and assemble his hit kit. He later would say that choosing another victim so close to his house (Hedge was the first) was a sign of "laziness" and that stalking so close to home isn't "something serial killers do."

After he clothed himself in the dark hit clothing or costume, he walked nearly two miles through the frigid Kansas December, through a large field and a cemetery to arrive at Davis' house. Her house was quite rural and secluded which also would play in Rader's favor regarding his penchant for protracted play with the dead bodies. Once Rader arrived at Davis' house, he was hesitant. It was dark outside so he could not gain entrance by faking his employment as a telephone repair person. This would have to be a break-in. But Rader didn't mind the chaos of a break-in scenario, as it would only increase his victim's fear. And his victims' fear fed him. Now, he cased Davis' house before, many times, but was always unable to find easy access to entry. So, when he arrived on the night he "selected," he's cold and frustrated as he walked around the house trying to figure out how to get in.

Rader: After spending some time at that residence—it was very cold that night. Had some reservations going in 'cause I had cased the place before, and I really couldn't figure out how to get in. She was in the house, so I finally just selected a-a concrete block and threw it through the window on the east side and came in.

Waller: All right. So you used this concrete block to break a window?

Rader: Mm-hmm. Plate glass window, patio door, mm-hmm.

Rader says that after he shattered the glass door, he simply stepped inside to see Dee Davis come out from her bedroom to sort out what that loud noise was. Rader says she told him she thought a car had hit her house. But he soon disabused her of this faulty thinking.

Rader: I told her that I was-I used a- the ruse of being wanted. I was on the run; I needed food, car, warmth, warm up.

Rader says that Davis took all of this information in quietly. Feeling comfortable with her compliance, he "handcuffed her and kind of talked to her, told her I would like to get some food, get her keys to her car…" As with other retellings, Rader placed himself in a position of benevolence. In his mind, he takes care of his victims. He is kind to them, taking time to reassure them that they will not be harmed. All the while, his victims are handcuffed or otherwise bound and have a gun in their faces. He says that with Davis he, "walked, talked with her a little bit and calmed her down a little bit."

Rader followed his usual modus operandi by going through her purse and house before committing the murder. He always secured his victims' ID and the car keys before taking the victim back to a bedroom. He does this for two reasons: one, he can increase the fear of the victim as he methodically takes claim to their possessions, and two, by securing the car keys before the murder, he has a quick and easy exit strategy.

Rader says that while Davis sat handcuffed, he toured her home, took her driver's license (which should have been a clue that he was gathering trophies), checked on the location of her car and even pretended to gather up food as if he was going to leave without further incident.

Rader: I went back and checked where the car was, simulated getting some food, odds and ends in the house [trophies], kind of like I was leaving, then went back and removed the handcuffs and-and then tied her up.

This is not the first time Rader opened his crime by handcuffing the victim, but the handcuffs are simply for show. Rader's fetishism requires fabric for the strangulation, preferably nylon. And that's exactly what he does here, with Davis. She was pleading with him not to harm her: "I've got kids, don't hurt me, don't hurt me." She kept crying. Rader said he talked with her "until she calmed down."

Rader has mentioned "calming down" his victims in nearly every interview and certainly in his confession. He posits this action in the light of his heroism. He seems to believe that his tenderness is a compassionate display. He feels like the good guy for taking time out his fantasized murder to assuage the terror in his victims. But he only attempts to "calm them down" for his own pleasures. Remember that Rader needs complete control; he does not like the victims who scream, fight or resist. So his "calming down" techniques are solely for his own gain. A calm victim produces a more intense orgasm for him during and after the actual strangulation.

So, here, with Davis, a woman of modesty, grace, and sincerity, according to her son, Jeff Davis, Rader played this "calming down" game. It is much like the poison a spider injects into its victims to paralyze or "calm" them so that the actual kill is easier for the predator. Rader said that he "removed the handcuffs and-and then tied her up [with fabric] and then-and then eventually strangled her." Rader used a pair of her pantyhose to perform the murder. But the murder didn't happen in the speed and efficiency in which Rader originally confessed. Judge Waller asks for more details.

Waller: All right. You say "eventually strangled her."

Rader: Well, after I tied her up. I went through some things in the room there, and then-and then strangled her.

This means that Davis was alive and alert after he secured her bindings. She was lying across her own bed, watching, listening to her "compassionate" soon-to-be murderer rifle through her personal, intimate belongings, all the while suspended in his time frame, his world, his sexual fantasy. Rader said it took three minutes to strangle her and those three minutes produced years of sexual pleasure for him afterwards.

After the murder, just as with Hedge, Rader moved her body to a blanket and dragged her to the trunk of her car. He was in a bit of a rush now because he needed to get back to the Boy Scout camp before he was missed. In his confession he says, "I really had a commitment I needed to go to…"

Once Davis' body was secure in her trunk, he drove her car to a nearby lake in Park City. He pulled her out of the trunk and superficially hid her under a thatch of trees. He pulled some foliage over her, but isn't overly concerned as he intended to come back at a later time. Once her body is secured, he drove back to her house, did his "right hand rule" clean-up, and took the items he found while going through her lingerie drawer while she lay in wait on her bed.

He then retraced his steps through the field and cemetery back to the Baptist Church where he has left his car. Here, he changed out of his hit clothes and back into his scout uniform. But he began to feel insecure about Davis' location under the trees by the lake. So, he drove his own car back there, uncovered her, dragged her on the blanket to his trunk, and finally left her body under a bridge in Sedgwick County.

From there he raced back to camp and played Boys Scout Leader for the remainder of the final night of the camp out. When Rader returned home, he drove back to the second location, under the bridge, where he "prettied her up" and placed a mask on her face. He is proud of this mask, telling police interrogator's, "That's my mask. I wear that mask too. I pose myself with this mask and you'll find those with my stash." That night, after the murder, he placed the mask over Dee's decomposing face and took pictures of her in various poses.

Later, using a remote cord, he dressed in the lingerie he stole from her, placed the mask on his own face, and posed in positions of bondage and strangulation. In one picture, he has buried himself up to his neck. The pictures show only his head above the earth and that mask on his face. Davis's body would not be found for thirteen more days. And it wouldn't be for another fourteen years before Jeff Davis could confront him in a courtroom to say, "I can think of nothing but savoring the bittersweet taste of revenge as justice is served upon this social sewage here before us today."

RADER'S CAPTURE AND ARREST

After he murdered Dolores Davis, Rader once again entered his cooling off period. He never intended for Davis to become his final victim, but because his ego demanded attention, he taunted the public at large and the police in particular. It would be his own hubris would lead to his capture.

But at first, and following his strict post-murder routine, Rader continued with his everyday life as a father and husband. He continued to be involved in his church, serving as the President of the Congregant up until his arrest. His day job was as a Park City Code Enforcement Officer which played in neatly with his trolling expeditions. As an enforcer, he was charged with encouraging the community residents to follow the guidelines for life in their neighborhoods. This included petty issues like the length of someone's lawn—and Rader was once seen kneeling down on a resident's lawn with a ruler in his hand to measure the length of grass—to rounding up dogs that had broken loose from their fences. The job was meant to be more carrot than stick, meaning the Code Enforcers were meant to serve as friendly reminders to the community outliers to step back into the harmony of the neighborhood. But Rader was particularly tough on his beat.

One woman was once cited by Rader for her dog being off a leash on public property. Rader cited her on four separate occasions. The woman decided to fight these tickets in court. Her attorney, Danny Seville, was shocked by the amount of detail and pettiness Rader included in the paperwork. He said, "[Rader] spent hours and hours and hours and days on just trying to prove these four tickets. I do criminal defense and I have major felony, you know, rape cases, and sometimes they don't have this amount of paperwork involved." Among the paperwork was a picture Rader had taken of the dog standing on the wrong side of the fence. Saville said that, "a normal compliance officer would open the gate and encourage the dog back into the yard and maybe look around for the breach in the fence to determine how it got out. But did Dennis do that? No, he was trying to shoot the dog with a tranquilizer gun."

Many have speculated that this type of control, this insistence on winning at any cost, played itself out in Rader's murderous fantasies. But to make the jump from hyper-litigious citations to a murderous serial killer? That jump was simply too large to bridge with common sense. Seville says, "I can see Dennis killing dogs, you know, he was trying to shoot Shadow [his client's dog] from the backyard. But I never thought that he would be the kind of person that would kill people."

By 2004, nearly thirteen years since Delores Davis' murder, the Wichita Eagle ran a story about the BTK speculating that the killer was either dead or imprisoned. They ran the story on the thirtieth anniversary of the Otero family slayings. This didn't sit well with egomaniacal Rader. He needed the public to know that he was alive and too clever for prison. And, more importantly, he needed to remind them that he was still walking among them. Rader's end game was always to increase fear. It bolstered his paper-thin ego.

Shortly after The Eagle published the article about him, Rader sent a letter to the editor claiming responsibility for the unsolved 1986 murder of Vicki Wegerle. Her widowed husband, Bill, was still seen as guilty for the murder, despite lack of evidence to even charge him. The paper published Rader's letter, but nothing further came of it. Richard LaMunyon, Chief of Police for Park City, falsely suspected that the BTK was opening communication with remorse or a sense of guilt for what he had done. LaMunyon couldn't have been more wrong. He later said, "I remember I was sitting here in my city office, my secretary said, 'Chief Williams is on the line and needs to talk to you.' So, I picked up the phone and he said 'Chief, you're not going to belief this, we just got a communication from BTK.'" LaMunyon was shocked, having been part of the force dedicated to catching this murderer for so many years. He said, "you've got to be kidding me." And when LaMunyon went down to the other chief's office, he knew it was BTK. He says, "My first reaction was, I thought maybe he was coming back, perhaps it was remorse, uh, regret that brought him back. But, but it just wasn't. It was arrogance. He's just evil."

Rader, feeling antsy and uncelebrated, began sending coded messages and even puzzles to The Eagle and other local news outlets. Nola Foulston from the District Attorney's Office said of Rader, "He started to play these little games, of sending us on scavenger hunts around the city, putting cereal boxes [all of Rader's packages were placed inside *cereal* boxes as a nod to the phonetic connect to his position as a *serial* killer] serial killer boxes filled with dolls that were posed in positions of victims, and pieces of jewelry from some of his victims. He would hide them in the city and then he would call the media and he'd send them a little note, a little clue where you might find these things." Foulston wondered at the magnitude of his games.

She considered, "His gamesmanship, was just, uh, I think he really wanted to get caught."

Randy Stone, a detective with the forensic computer crimes unit, felt certain that Rader's frequency of contact would soon lead to his arrest. He said, "There was a lot of confidence that if he kept going, we would eventually catch him." There were so many detectives assigned to the BTK case that Stone thought, "Everybody in the department, I'm sure, to some extent, hoped to be the one to find that magic bullet that would find him." Indeed, the prosecutors and the detectives were baffled at Rader's overconfidence. Foulston said, "He was doing things that were stupid, and law enforcement were gaining a lot of perspective into this individual."

In this flurry of cat and mouse gamesmanship, Rader substantiated his claim as being the BTK by inserting pieces of evidence he had tucked away in one of his hidey holes. He didn't limit his taunting to just the victims' jewelry. He would sometimes include their driver's license and or even polaroid photos he took during the actual crime.

This kind of exchange went on for just about a year, and while Rader thought he was the cat toying with the mouse, Rader disastrously underestimated his "mouse." Detective Ken Landwehr, a Sedgwick County Homicide Detective was no mouse. Detective Landwehr strategically outwitted Rader at his own game. Landwehr began to build a relationship of sorts with Rader. Rader would send coded messages through news outlets and Landwehr would decipher them and respond. His sole aim was to keep the BTK talking, keep him captivated by his own so-called brilliance. Landwehr was certain that the BTK would make a mistake. And Landwehr was patient. He was a cool cat, slowly, very slowly drawing the BTK into his confidence even as he was prepared to pounce.

And a year after sending his letter to the Wichita Eagle, Rader made his first mistake. He wrote to a local television station asking them to investigate a package he allegedly left at the local Home Depot on North Woodlawn. But Rader hadn't actually left the package inside the store, but rather in the back of a pick-up truck parked in the Home Depot parking lot. It belonged to a Home Depot employee. But the employee never even saw the package. It was his girlfriend who discovered it several days later, and when she showed her boyfriend, they opened it to discover a cereal box with several documents with poorly spelled words and appalling grammar seeming to discuss murder. But the young couple just thought the whole thing was a joke and threw it away. It wasn't until the police began asking questions at his work that the Home Depot employee mentioned the mysterious package from the back of his truck. Fortunately, the police were able to retrieve the package from his home trash can.

Among the documents found within the discarded package were detailed plans for future murders, a gold chain, a handful of 3X5 index cards, a copied photo from a book detailing a killer who bound and gagged his victims and, of course, the much-discussed question about the security of a floppy disk. As was his penchant, Rader had used an old cereal box to package his treasures. The question Rader asked of Landwehr was if it was safe, if it was secure for him to send a floppy disk to communicate with the police. The document read that if the BTK could not be traced through a floppy disk, Landwehr was to place an ad in the local paper with the message, "Rex, it will be okay." Landwehr was more than happy to post the lie. And Rader took the bait. Two weeks after the "Rex" ad was placed, on the 16th of February

2005, the police department received what was to become his final correspondence to the police. Rader sent this final missive to the KSAS-TV station in Wichita who immediately phoned the police.

When Landwehr turned the evidence over to his forensic computer detective, Randy Stone, the opened the disk read only, "This is a test." It then posted directions for the police to refer to the 3X5 index cards from his previous package, the one found in the pick-up truck, for instructions on how to proceed with the communications. Rader, sitting in his suburban home, faithfully serving his church every Sunday and loving his wife and children throughout the week, felt he was king supreme sitting in his lair, spinning a web for the police. Rader was amusing himself.

But Stone was good at his game as well. He said, "I opened it up; there was one file and from that we were able to identify that the person who last saved the document was logged into his computer under the account name of 'Dennis'."

And Landwehr was having some fun of his own. He scoured the Home Depot security cameras until he found the time and date that Rader dropped off the package in the employee's pick-up truck bed. The cameras were not close enough to distinguish any features on the unidentified man seen leaving a package in the back of the truck. However, they very clearly depicted a black Grand Cherokee pulling up to the truck and then showed the driver of the Cherokee getting out and surveilling the truck. So now Landwehr had a make and model of the BTK's car.

Additionally, Stone was still gathering information from the floppy disk. While the content itself was limited to just the one line about the test and to look at the index cards for more instructions, in the property's menu of the disk, it showed that the disk had been saved by a "Dennis." So now there was the car and there was a first name. Forensic computer experts were also able to trace the geographic locations the disk had traveled in its inauspicious life. They now knew that the disk had been used at the Park City Library and at one other location.

It would be this second location that would end the BTK's reign of dread in Kansas. The disk had been used inside the Christ Lutheran Church. In fact, the software used to create the file was registered to Christ Lutheran Church. Stone said that Rader had taken some precautions to mar the identity of the disk, but his mistake was taking it to the church to use in their computers. Rader later told police that his home printer was out of order, so he took the disk to the church to print out the file. Landwehr said, "It's pretty basic stuff. Anybody who knows anything about computers could figure it out." Once they had the name of the church, it was just a matter of a couple of clicks to get to a picture and name of the president of their congregation. Dennis Rader's name was printed under a picture of his smiling face.

District Attorney Foulston remembers the shock in the law enforcement community when it was determined that Dennis Rader, a leader in the Lutheran church and Boy Scout Volunteer was the BTK. She said, "We were like 'Oh my God' and then that's when everything just started to move very, very, very rapidly."

The police easily determined his employment with Park City as a Code Compliance Officer and very quickly discovered his address. Landwehr drove past his house at 6220 Independence Street, Park City, Kansas. The name of the street would mock Rader's future. In the driveway sat a black Grand Cherokee which was registered in his son Brian's name. It was an identical match to the Grand Cherokee seen in the Home Depot surveillance videos.

Now, Landwehr wanted to move carefully. Should he rush this arrest or miss even a basic step, he might trample Rader's civic rights and therefore let him off on a technicality. And he was not going to let this happen. Because he could not openly ask Dennis Rader for a sample of his DNA without tipping their hand, Landwehr instead subpoenaed Rader's daughter Kerri's DNA from a pap smear done five years previously, when she was student at Kansas State University. And the wait for the results was scary. Foulston said, "They didn't have everything they needed at that point to take him into custody, so you'd be leaving a guy out there with his DNA sample hanging out. And he was not inactive. He continued to plan homicides up until the day we caught him."

So, the entire department was on edge, waiting for those lab results. The lab was busy comparing Kerri Rader's DNA to the DNA collected at the numerous crime scenes including a sample nearly thirty years old, taken from 12-year-old Josephina Otero's legs. Finally, the lab sent the news to Landwehr. Kerri's DNA was a familial match to the biological crime scene evidence. Landwehr now had sufficient cause to issue an arrest warrant.

So, on an ordinary Friday, just as he was preparing to have his lunch break at noon, Dennis Rader's car was stopped near his house and where he was arrested and charged with ten murders. It was February 25, 2005 and his thirty-year span of terror and murder was finished. The BTK was finally in custody.

While he was being handcuffed, the arresting officer asked him if he knew why he was being arrested. Rader replied, "Oh, I have my suspicions why."

When Landwehr entered the interrogation room, Rader was stunned. He "couldn't get over the fact" that Landwehr had lied to him about the culpability of the floppy disk, and Rader was angry about this deception. He fancied himself the con man, the spy, the clever puppeteer. That Landwehr had played *him* enraged Rader. But Rader, ever the narcissist, couldn't bear to be brought down by a mere mortal man. He blamed the floppy disk saying, "the floppy did me in." Rader's bail was set at 10 million dollars.

THE POLICE INTERROGATIONS

Dennis Rader's police interrogation would last 33 hours over the course of two days and fill 17 DVDs. The length was not due to the police wearing Rader down. Rader openly and eagerly confessed to the murders, detailing each with astonishing pride. When asked if he felt anything for the victims, Rader responds, "I mean, I have a lot of feelings for them. I guess it's more of an achievement for this object in the hunt. Or sort of more of a high, I guess."

Near the beginning of the interrogation, Rader continued his cat and mouse game, believing himself to be the most clever man in the room. But the police patiently laid out their case before him, and even Rader knew he was defeated. It took only three hours, almost to the minute, into the interrogation for Rader to confess.

He leaned forward with his chin resting in his hand and said, "I guess you guys got me. What else can I say?" The detective jumped in and tells Rader to, "say, say who you are," to which Rader replied, "I'm BTK." Landwehr immediately pushed over an evidence bag with the purple floppy disk inside asking Rader, "do you know what this is?" Rader is visibly shaken by the evidence. He began forcefully poking his finger on it, repeatedly pounding his finger on top of the disk and asked, "I need to ask you. Why the hell did you lie to me?" Rader was still angry about Landwehr's deceit. Rader continued to punch the bag with his finger, as if for emphasis, and said again, "How can you lie to me?" To which Landwehr calmly, almost coolly replied, "Because I was trying to catch you."

During the police interrogation, Rader commented to Clint Snyder, a Wichita Detective, that he was sorry for his callous manner in describing his victims, often referring to their near-death pleas as "yada, yada, yada." Apparently, Radar read a look of astonishment on Snyder's face when he attempted to explain his indifference toward his victims, "I'm sorry, I know this is a human being [we are talking about], but I'm a monster." Another detective in the room, Kelly Otis, remembered Rader's demeanor as cavalier. "It was like we were talking over coffee, as if he were relaying a fishing story," she recalled.

After his lengthy confessions, the Police Chief called for a press conference—and the community was riveted. The media told their viewers that at the upcoming press conference, they would reveal the BTK's identity. Local resident and former classmate of Rader's, Roger Farthing, said he told his wife to come get him "when they make the announcement." He said he went out to work on his son's car when his wife came out to tell him, "the guy's name was Dennis Rader."

Farthing said, "I almost fell into the car. I just couldn't believe it." Farthing, along with Rader, always attended their class reunions. Farthing said, "we always took a group photo, and we were all there at our fortieth high school reunion which was shorty before he was arrested." Farthing said that he and his wife were seated across from Rader and his wife, Paula, and that, "we carried on quite a conversation, it was a very enjoyable evening. You just can't believe that you misread somebody this bad for so long."

Even Dennis Rader's own defense attorney, Steve Osburn, was shocked by Dennis Rader's comportment. He claims, "I've lost track of how many murderers I've defended over the years. He's not even in my top ten of people that I would consider dangerous, just by how you meet them and talk with them. I've had other people that just exude meanness and fear; it's like 'this guy, I don't even want to be in the same room with him.' But not Dennis. I mean, I didn't get that from him. I think that's why he was able to go so long, because, when he wasn't actually doing his acts, he had this persona, aura of normality that nobody suspected that he could be a killer."

Professor David Wilson works as a criminologist and he explains that Rader's eagerness to help the police, and even his demeanor at his sentencing hearing, was simply a display of pride. "In his warped, immoral worldview, behaving as he has done, killing all these people, is something that he should be proud of, not ashamed of. And that's why he's so keen to help police, and that's why he's so keen to talk about these things at court. Not because he's ashamed but because he's proud," Wilson said. And this analysis of Rader's crimes runs in accordance with the general psychological community who research such phenomena, including Dr. Katherine Ramsland, mentioned in earlier sections of this book.

Ramsland agrees with Professor Wilson's diagnosis of Rader's pride. But Ramsland goes a step deeper to argue that Dennis Rader was not "born to kill." She said, "I don't think there is an evil seed there, that bloomed and inevitably forced his hand. I definitely think it was series of orgasmic conditioning that could have gone a different way."

And this consensus of Rader's culpability is even shared by his own defense attorney, Osburn: "Given the fact that there doesn't seem to be any [lack of] nurture, you have to say the fault was inside him. I just don't think you can kill ten people and be sane. There is something seriously wrong with your inner workings if you are able to kill people, especially children, and to do some of things that he did, and just continuing functioning. Like go on with your life like nothing else is wrong."

Certainly Rader's "broken inner workings" were on full display at his plea hearing. Rader was not to have a trial because he proudly pled "guilty" to all charges. But his guilty plea changed quickly. At his arraignment on May 3, 2005, Rader refused to speak and so the judge entered a "not guilty" plea for each of the ten counts. This court plea entering is standard procedure for defendants who refuse to enter one their own behalf. Perhaps Rader still felt he was in complete control of his universe.

If so, it would only take less than a month sitting in a jail cell, wearing his orange jumpsuit—a far cry from his notorious "kill clothes"—and under the scrutiny and commands of his jailers, that Rader would change his plea to "guilty." On June 27, 2005, at his pre-arranged hearing, Rader was almost gleeful in his plea change and captivated the courtroom and a generous audience around the world with his stoic rendition of his deeds.

Normal procedure would dictate that Rader would not speak or present any evidence at this hearing, as it was a formality to enter a plea. But nothing about Rader was normal, including his plea hearing. Because of the unique nature of his crimes and considering the span and reach of both time and number of victims, the state allowed

Rader's testimony to be presented at his plea hearing. This decision was made in the most part, with Rader's victims' families in mind. They were to be given time and space at his sentencing hearing later, to directly confront Rader about how he had destroyed their lives. The court felt that by allowing Rader a time to publicly explain his crimes, it might help the victims' families to heal.

But this hearing was to be the "Rader Show," with Rader controlling even this punitive phase of his crimes. On June 27, 2005, at 9:01 am, in a courtroom inside the Sedgwick County Courthouse, Dennis Rader spoke with Judge Waller with a gallery packed with his victims' families and members of the press. A notable absence in the audience was Rader's own wife, Paula. On June 26, a day before his plea hearing, Paula requested an emergency divorce from her 34-year-old marriage on claims of emotional distress. Sedgwick County District Judge, Eric Yost, waived the mandatory 60 day waiting period and granted the divorce as final the very day she requested it.

Paula Rader would change her name back to Paula Dietz. She would never visit him in prison nor attend any of his hearings. Dietz has never made a public statement regarding her former husband. But if her absence affected Rader, he certainly didn't show it. And with a packed courtroom and more spectators clustered outside, Dietz' decision to not attend went largely unnoticed.

Rader's defense attorney opened the spectacle by informing Judge Waller that "Mr. Rader would waive his rights to a jury trial and enter a plea of guilty to all ten charges." There were some formalities after this statement, with District Attorney Foulston entering her name into record, but the courtroom held its breath, waiting for the main event. All eyes were focused on Dennis Rader's back. Judge Waller then went through the ten counts, listing each murder by its date and the name of the victim and adding at the end of each count, "Sir, do you understand that you are charged with Murder in the First Degree, a Class A Felony?" to which Rader responded, "Yes sir." Rader would repeat this phrase ten times until all ten victims were put into the record.

Once the court business is concluded, the judge reminds Rader that he is constitutionally permitted to a jury by trial. He painstakingly explains this process to Rader including instructions like, "if there was a trial the state would bring witnesses to court…" and, "your attorneys would have the right to question every witness called by the state and in that way, confront those people for you." The judge would ask Rader, "do you understand that?" every so often in this laborious explanation of criminal justice. Rader dully responded to the judge with a solemn "Yes, sir" after every question.

The judge then read the entire Defendant's Acknowledgment of Rights and Entry of Plea form. The DA bristles at some of the wording, but Waller assures her that she can readdress these issues at sentencing. After reading Rader's form, Waller questioned Rader's understanding of the form. "Did you have an opportunity to go over this form thoroughly with your lawyer?" To which Rader answers with the obvious, "Yes, sir, many times," in that Rader filled the form out with his attorney shortly before this hearing.

But the judge, perhaps worried of an appeal, presses Rader even further, asking, "Are you pretty much assured that you understand each and every one of your rights in this case?" Rader responds with, "Yes, sir. The defense worked with me real well. We went over them, and, you know, I ---I feel like I'm pretty happy with it. Ready to go." Rader wanted to skip ahead to the part where he could boast to a captive audience the details of his darkest deeds. But the judge was a stickler for rule and order, and so the administrative parade continued.

Waller: If you enter a plea of guilty, you would give up many of your appeal rights because you would not be able to appeal. For example, a factual basis. You will have the right, however, to appeal the manner in which the proceedings have been completed and done up to this point.

Rader: Okay.

For eight more pages of transcript, Judge Waller, determined to hold his courtroom to the highest legal standard, continued to explain the legal process to Rader. Then, finally:

Waller: All right, Mr. Rader, at this time, I'm going to ask you how you plead to all ten counts?

Rader: Guilty.

Waller: Are you pleading guilty because you are guilty or are you pleading guilty for another reason?

Rader: Yes, sir.

Waller then explains to Rader that he will reread each count and offer Rader the chance to explain his actions that prove him guilty.

Waller: In regards to Count One, please, tell me in your own words what you did on the 15th day of January, 1974 in Sedgwick County, Kansas that makes you believe you are guilty of Murder in the First Degree.

And so, it began. And for the next two days, Rader gleefully recounted each murder with robotic detail and barely suppressed pride. All of the murders were accounted for and Rader was able to explain his clever role in each of his "projects." At the end of his "hit parade," Rader stands quietly before the judge.

Waller: All right, so all of these instances, these ten counts occurred because you wanted to satisfy a sexual fantasy, is that correct?

Rader: Yes, mm-hmm.

The judge then asks Rader to be seated and there is a collective exhale from the gallery. Judge Waller then moved to the adjudication.

Waller: …based on your statements to this court, I will find there are factual basis for each of these pleas of "guilty." I will accept these pleas and adjudge you, Dennis Rader, guilty of Murder in the First Degree, in Count One, A Class A Felony, Guilty of Murder in the First Degree, in Count Two, A Class A Felony…

And so it went, each life that Rader stole was reduced to a count in a murder trial, each victim becoming a reductive version of themselves. In that courtroom, they became only what Rader made them. They became victims. At one point in the proceedings, standing there in his tan suit wearing a dark tie, Rader tried to explain his craft to Judge Waller. He intimated that he was an accomplished serial killer referring to other serial killers as "my kind of person." He told the judge that serial killers like him behave in organized and logical ways. He kindly detailed the stages or phases serial killers go through including "trolling," "stalking," and then ended his teaching session with this sobering statement. "They become the victim, or, at least, that's what you want them to become."

And, in Rader's courtroom, all ten of the humans he murdered became just that. They became his victims. Their names would always be joined with his and this delighted Rader. They were, after all, *his* victims. But Rader was not to have the last word after all. His sentencing hearing was scheduled for 21 days later, and here, the families would finally have a voice.

Rader was taken back to the county jail to wait for his next court appearance, and the four prosecuting lawyers and eight county detectives used the time to prepare for their own parade of evidence. Because no evidence was presented at his plea hearing, the prosecution would get its chance to highlight the crimes, including power point slides and physical evidence to help secure the sentencing in their favor. Rader was not eligible for the death penalty because his final murder of Delores Davis was committed three years before Kansas reinstated the death penalty. Rader himself was disappointed by this ruling. He claimed, "I thought if I ever had to be put away, I wanted to be hung, but I guess they don't do that anymore."

The Sentencing Hearing

Detective Landwehr and his dedicated team of officers and the prosecution team headed by Nola Foulston were eager to present evidence. They understood, of course, that this wouldn't be a trial, but rather a way to appeal to the judge that Rader's sentencing should run consecutively and concurrently. The prosecution was afraid that if Waller ruled to run Rader's sentence concurrently, Rader may one day be eligible for parole. This parole issue had to do with Dolores Davis' murder. Rader committed this crime in 1991 and by this time, Kansas state laws had shifted in such a way as to allow for parole in a murder charge. The prosecutors needed to convince the judge of Rader's unassailable wickedness and prove that this wickedness could not be rehabilitated.

Because most of the prosecution team had worked the Rader case for decades, they were very well aware of Rader's hubris. They knew that by presenting a detailed case, revisiting each crime in detail and with forensic thoroughness, Rader would be egoistically and sexually charged. Foulston explained this by saying, "Sometimes you have to feed the dragon before you can put its fire out." She considered their decision to allow Rader access to crime scene photos, and the physical evidence, knowing it might produce what Rader calls "sparky big time," referring to sexual stimulation even unto climax. Her job was to secure Rader in a prison cell for the rest of his natural life and if she had to dance with the devil to make this happen, then turn up the music.

Despite Rader's shocking account of his ten murders roughly three weeks earlier, especially the detail and recall he presented at his plea hearing, the public nor the victim's families were prepared for what was in store during the next seven hours of the sentencing hearing. Rader's admissions suddenly felt like Disney movie to the sordid 'for mature audiences only' courtroom display.

And it was a detailed display. This detail was, in part, due to Rader's own fascination with his crimes. From his two-day confessional to the detectives, to his years of taunting the police and the community with his cereal box packages, as well as his now officially-recorded rendition at the plea hearing, provided the prosecution with an astonishing amount of evidence. Because Rader was so meticulous in the telling, Foulston was able to tell the court the thirty-year long story, punctuating the picture with hundreds of pieces of evidence.

For example, when discussing Shirley Vian Wegerle's murder, the attorney pulled a plastic airplane, a firetruck, and a toy van out of an evidence bag to show the court what her three children were given to play with while they were imprisoned in the bathroom, both hearing and seeing their mother be stripped, bound and strangled. These types of details in symphony with the visual artifacts turned the courtroom into a macabre theater. Add to this visual acuity Rader's penchant for chattiness, and the prosecutors were able to insert Rader's own words into their case. Rader, for example, told detectives at his interrogation that after the Otero family murders, he realized he did not have the strength he needed to strangle a human in such a way as to produce the highest sexual charge he was seeking. So, after his disappointing strangling of Julie Otero, and then his frustration with Josephina's long hair interfering with his attempts to strangle her while she was suspended by the basement pipes, he decided to do strength exercises by using a stress ball. He would squeeze the ball throughout his workday to better prepare himself for the next murder. And that was always Rader's sick game, to get to the next murder.

Some argued that the prosecution went too far when showing still photographs of the dead victims. Tongues were protruded, eyes swollen shut, and two of the victims were in a state of advanced decay. But the prosecution marched forward with confidence despite the gruesome story they told with such clarity. Some of the victim's pictures were so intense that Rader himself averted his eyes when they were displayed on the courtroom monitor.

At Rader's arrest and then again during his police confession, Rader told Landwehr of a "mother lode" of evidence he kept stored in various locations. One of the locations, in fact the one hidey hole he stored the bulk of his treasures in, was inside a locked filing cabinet door inside the Christ Lutheran Church. This drawer contained victims' stolen underwear, news clippings of his crimes, and polaroid shots of him wearing the undergarments in various positions of strangulation. One of the pictures details Rader "hanging" upside down in Dolores Davis' bra and underwear with his smug face hidden behind the very mask he had placed on her naked body, which he also photographed.

The police gathered wheelbarrow loads of evidence from multiple hidey holes. Rader claimed to have had so many he couldn't remember all of their locations. But this seems unlikely given Rader's precision and detailed recall. It's more believable that he kept a few of the hidey holes to himself so that, even from his isolated prison cell, he could imagine their contents and enjoy their secrecy as his own private collection.

Among items recovered, the police found his personal sketches he drew with alarming detail of his victims, always naked, always bound, always under his control. They also uncovered an unfinished manuscript Rader was working on. He said his plan was to have it published at his death. He titled it, "The BTK Story." And so, the evidence table was burdened with the mountains of physical evidence he himself had preserved.

And during these long, heated seven hours, Rader stood sentry over his deeds; in his view, he sat in the seat of honor, interpreting the prosecution's case more as an award show to his accomplishments. And the families sitting behind him? The court proceedings were interrupted multiple times with the quiet sobs of a surviving son or mother.

This prolonged parade of the minutia, this gory account of Rader's past thirty years, swelled the emotions of the families until they were nearly bursting to have their turn at the microphone. What they couldn't understand from their position of righteous anger, is that nothing they could say to Rader would affect him in any way other than to stroke his ego. Indeed, Rader would consider hurled insults and demonstrative weeping as evidence of fandom. The outrage and pain presented by each speaker? It fed him: he received their sorrow and rage as precious gifts.

But the prosecution was still not finished, so the courtroom held its collective breath, listening to words and viewing ordinary household items like a radio or a pair of pantyhose as cherished relics, the last known objects to connect a loved one to a lost one. When Lieutenant Ken Landwehr took the stand, the energy shifted in the courtroom. Here was an experienced professional who had dedicated a large chunk of his career to capturing the BTK. That it took him nearly thirty years was forgiven, because the public was just so relieved that Rader had been arrested and the era of BTK was over.

Foulston asked Landwehr why this particular case was different from all of his previous murder cases, including other serial killers.

Landwehr: In this case we had a long time between victims and deaths, we had a killer that writing us and also writing the media outlets and was selective, it appears, in choosing his victims.

Landwehr was assigned to the BTK task force after seven of the victims were already dead. But Landwehr's tenacious efforts were threatening enough for the BTK to take notice. During his testimony, in fact, Landwehr stated that when Rader was initially arrested and placed into his car, his first words were, "Hello Mr. Landwehr." Foulston takes a successful swing at Rader when she asks Landwehr about Rader fostering a comradery with him regarding their professions in law enforcement.

Foulston: Mr. Rader commented about the fact that he felt a lot of camaraderie with you…He felt pretty good about it because, after all, he said that he felt he was a law enforcement officer and that you were too. Well, Mr. Rader's not a law enforcement officer, he's dog catcher.

Rader, sitting in a stark gray suite with a patterned dark gray tie, clenches his jaw and looks down during this exchange. Once the prosecution had finished their case—and it was long, not just because of the amount of evidence they presented, but because they had to account for ten humans and the special circumstances surrounding their murders—the victims were finally given a chance to speak. Rader appeared emotionless but for one brief wiping of his eyes at one of the statements given. The victims were placed deep into the aisle of the gallery, behind Rader. The court had set up a microphone and a stool for them to read their statements. Charlie Otero, son of Joseph and Julie Otero, who found their bodies after coming home from school, opened the comments. He spoke of how close-knit the family is now. He esteemed his sister and remaining brother, speaking of their unbreachable connection.

Charlie: As far as I'm concerned, when it is all done, Dennis Rader has failed in his effort to kill the Otero's.

Charlie spoke for just over two minutes and held the courtroom captive with his gentle manner and soft voice. His sister was next to speak, and she arrived to the microphone with visible anger. She told Rader that, "we have never met before, but you have seen my face before. It is the same face you murdered over thirty years ago. The face of my mother, Julie Otero."

The court ordered the victim impact statement speakers in order of the crimes Rader had committed. This put Kevin Bright, one of Rader's few survivors, up next. Tall, thin, and humble, Kevin spoke of the struggle he fought against Rader in his sister's house that day. "The only thing I wish had been different that when I wrestled the gun from him… that it would have gone off and that would have been the end there."

Steve Relford, Shirley Vian Relford's son, came forward next. He was three years old at the time of the murder and sat in his living room while his mother was bound and tortured upstairs. He was crying before he even reached the microphone. Wiping away tears, he said that he hadn't prepared anything for this moment. He did not speak from notes. He spoke for less than a minute saying, "I just hope he will suffer for the rest of his life." He started to add "You know, I" but was unable to complete his sentence, waved his hand in the air and said, "that's all," and turned to walk to the back of the courtroom.

Nancy Fox's older brother, Fred, spoke next. He had a commanding voice, steady and strong. He told the court that, "I hope his sentence is the worst it can be and that he can be put away from the rest of his life." He thanked the court and turned away from the microphone. Fred and Nancy's sister, Beverly Platt, approached the microphone and with a quavering voice, read from a legal pad. She began by telling the court how much she loved her sister, saying there just weren't enough words to explain her loss. She spoke slowly because of the sobs in her throat.

Beverly: Nancy's death is like a deep wound that will never, ever heal. As far as I'm concerned, Dennis Rader does not deserve to live. I want him to suffer as much as he made his victims suffer. But then, when I think about that, in his sick, perverted way, he'd probably find that as some kind of pleasure or reward. This man needs to be thrown in a deep, dark hole and left to rot. He should never see the light of day."

She broke from her notes here and looked up to the Judge and to Rader saying, "And I have some afterlife scenarios. Nancy, and all of his victims will be waiting with God and watching him as he burns in hell." She stifled a sob as she walked away from the microphone.

Rod Hook, in a pale pink shirt, stood forward facing with no notes. He told the court he was representing the family of Marine Hedge. There was a twelve second pause as he looked down, clearly trying to compose himself before speaking. When he looked back up, he said, "I only ask the court to provide the maximum sentence, allowed by law, to this monster that created this." And at "this" he circled his hand around the courtroom where many people were crying, and all were held in suspension of the Dennis Rader's dirty deeds. He then thanked the task force. He turned elegantly and walked to the back of the courtroom.

Bill Wegerle was next, and he was visibly upset. His name had only recently been cleared when Rader confessed to the murder of his wife, Vicki. He told the court that the past weeks had revealed Dennis Rader for what he was. He felt there could never be true justice and told the court, "There is no justice that you can exact upon him that will satisfy our needs. We can just ask the court to bestow upon him the most that you can. And, hopefully, we will not have to deal with him, or

hear from him or see him again.

Vicki and Bill's daughter, Stephanie Kline, spoke on behalf of herself and her brother, Brandon saying, "Don't let this monster have any comforts as he lives out his remaining years in prison. He isn't worthy."

The judge called Jeff Davis to the microphone. He is the son of Dolores Davis, Rader's final victim. He introduced himself by name and then invoked his mother's memory by telling the court her death date. "My name is Jeffery Davis, son of Dolores Davis, BTK victim, January 18, 1991." He spent some time offering condolences and shared grief with the other victims' families. He said he held hope that they could all "leave this courtroom with some sense of peace and legal resolution. For the last 5,326 days, I have wondered what it would be like to confront the walking cesspool that took my mother's precious life. He went on to say that he envisioned this day as one to avenge the past, as he relished the bittersweet taste of revenge confronting "social sewage here before us today." He called Rader a

"depraved predator, a rabid animal that has murdered people, poisoned countless lives and terrorized this community for thirty years. All the while, relishing every minute of it. As such, there can be no justice harsh enough or revenge bitter enough in this world, at least, to cause the pain and suffering this social malignancy has coming. Therefore, I have determined for the sake of our innocent victims and their loving families and friends here with us today, for me, this will be a day of celebration, not retribution. If my focus were hatred, I would stare you down and call you a demon from hell who defiles this court at the very sight of its cancerous presence. If I embraced bitterness, I would remind you that you are nothing more than a child-murdering, cowardly, impotent, eunuch and pervert, masquerading as a human being."

He went on to list all the things that Rader is, including "despicable" and "vile." He ended his laudable speech by saying, "in the final analysis, you have to live with the cold reality that all of us here will overcome your depravity. You have now lost everything, and you will forever remain [pause] nothing. May that torment you for the rest of your tortured existence."

At the close of victim impact statements, inexplicably, Dennis Rader was permitted to have the last word. He was granted audience with the judge and gallery to respond to the victims. Because the victim statements were considered aggravators, meaning they would influence the judge negatively toward sentencing, Rader was permitted a chance to mitigate their influence by responding to their statements.

Rader spoke for a rambling twenty minutes and housed his arrogance and pride in his accomplishment within words meaning to depict sorrow and humility. He admitted to selfishness, blaming his sexual predilections on what he calls "Factor X" in the courtroom but later calls "a demon." He appears to get choked up when apologizing to his family for "lying and cheating," which provides a glimpse into his mindset if he considers rape and murder as "cheating" on his wife. Again, Rader forces the victim to become a coconspirator in his crimes against them.

Rader went on to list the similarities he shares with his victims. He mentions that Stephanie Bright liked to spend time at her grandparent's farm. So did Rader. He says that he and Bright went to the same high school. He mentions Dolores Davis' love for animals which he claims he shares with her. This was a head scratcher to the gallery considering he so proudly discussed hanging and torturing animals during his plea hearing. He mentioned his neighbor Marine Hedge who loved to garden. Rader told the court that he, too, loved to garden.

When he mentioned Julie Otero, his connection feels foul in that he connects the two of them by saying, "Julie Otero looks a lot like my wife, Paula." It was a strange thing to say for many reasons, but among them, Paula was now his ex-wife. There was also the fact that he told the detectives that his interest in the Otero's was 12-year-old Josephina. Rader cleverly omits linking Josephina to his own daughter, Kerri.

He lists other victims and tries to convince the court how he is like them, but when he gets to Vicki Wegerle, his human mask slips, and he fully reveals the narcissist who runs the show. "Probably of all the people [meaning his victims], I didn't know Vicki Wegerle very much, although, I walked by her place [stalking her] and listened to the piano. I appreciate music." And suddenly, Rader shifts the attention from Vicki to himself by adding, as if it had any place in this context, "That's one thing I always wanted to learn was piano."

Apparently, he didn't want to learn how not to murder people.

When Rader finishes his list of *touching connections* between himself and the victims, he adds, "I hope I didn't leave anybody out," revealing that he was so distanced from discussing them that he couldn't be bothered to make certain that all ten of his victims were honored. But his statements weren't honoring anyway. They were just convenient ways to talk more about himself.

Rader did repeat the phrase "there is no way I can get out of this" three times in his wildly ranging speech. He seemed to want to make certain that he didn't miss a loophole somewhere. Rader's arrest and hearings only served to glorify him, in his thinking, but he was not as interested in the punitive effect of his confessions. He seemed to be frantically running paths through his brain to find a way out of the prison sentence awaiting him. He wanted to accept the infamy without the consequences.

Rader ended his sputtering, sometimes inaudible speech by offering the task force what they call their "academy awards." Rader spoke like a presenter at an award ceremony, naming detectives, the judge, and even his jailors as he commended each of them as "dedicated and hardworking...during all those great years." One assumes Rader refers to his thirty years of impunity as a terrorist murder as "those great years."

Rader asked the court for permission to keep some pictures of his family from his wallet and that the profits from the sale of his family home not go to cover court costs but rather to his "innocent wife." Rader quoted lines from poems, verses from the Bible, and ultimately ended his 27-minute speech with: "We speak of a man as an evil man; a dark side was there, but now I think light is beginning to shine."

Rader sat at the judge's request, and Foulston then has the final word to summarize the case and the charges against him, hoping for consecutive life terms, the maximum Judge Waller can impart. Foulston takes her time and speaks longer than the victims and Rader combined. When she is reaching her conclusions, she asks the court for special accommodations that would prohibit Rader from possessing, "receiving or creating any hand-written or computer-generated documents that describe sexual or murderous fantasies or intent." She wants the court to ban his access to writing or drawing material, or access to books or magazines that would "enflame his sexual appetite." When she finished speaking, there was some court chatter between Osburn, the judge and Foulston, but once that was cleared, Judge Waller asked Dennis Rader to stand.

Waller: In regards to Count One, it will be the judgment, order and sentence of the court that you, Dennis L. Rader be taken by the sheriff of Sedgwick County, Kansas and by hand delivered to the custody of the Secretary of Corrections to serve a term of life for the murder of Joseph Otero.

And so it went, from Count One all the way to Count Ten, that Rader was sentenced a full life term in exchange for each life he took. He would not be eligible for parole in forty years as the law allowed in Delores Davis' murder, and further, his sentence was to run consecutively.

Dennis Rader was escorted from the courtroom under the custody of the sheriff's department and later transferred to his current location at the El Dorado Correctional Facility in restrictive custody. This means he is isolated 23 hours a day and let out into a small room to exercise and shower one hour each weekday. The remaining two days a week he is kept in solitary confinement.

At last, Rader was officially captured and convicted. His daughter, Kerri, whose DNA helped to convict him, wrote a book several years into her father's incarceration. She examines the aftereffects her father's crimes had on her family and named her book *A Serial Killer's Daughter: My Story of Faith, Love and Overcoming*. In the book she writes, "I was born in '78. My father murdered a young woman when my mom was three months pregnant with me."

She also reveals how she was informed about her father's identity. She had been awakened by the sound of someone entering her apartment. "It was a normal day. I had taken the day off [as a substitute teacher]. I'm already…uptight thinking, 'who is this person in my apartment building' and then he said he was FBI." Once she was awake the agent asked her if she had heard of the BTK and, being from

Kansas, of course she had. He replied, "Your dad has been arrested as the BTK."

Rader has not remained out of the spotlight as his victims' families would have hoped. In 2009, he gave an interview to the Daily Mail saying he was "the facility's pet." Of his living accommodations, he boasted that he had "a nice window, a full metal door with a porthole window" and that inside his room he owned a "TV, radio and a hotpot." Despite Rader's attempts to bolster his sad life in prison, his inglorious reign as the BTK has ended, and his world is reduced to nothing more than a handful of possessions and hours of time for him to sit alone and do nothing—for the rest of his life.

BIBLIOGRAPHY

Author not named. Dennis Rader, Biography. Biography.com. February 14, 2020. Web.

Author not named. *Dennis Rader.* Criminal Minds. ND. Web

Beeman, Amy. *Inside Dennis Rader's Childhood: What Made Him the BTK Killer?* Heavy. May 24, 2021. Web.

Conroy, J. Oliver. *What Makes a Serial Killer?* The Guardian. August 10, 2018. Web.

Effron, Laura and Smith, Jennifer. *BTK Serial Killer's Daughter says she, her family are 'embracing a new start' since memoir released.* ABC News. July 25, 2019. Web.

Frie, Terry. Greely Resident/Author Jeff Davis, son of BTK killer's final victim blasts 20/20 documentary. Greely Tribune. February 1, 2019. Web.

Haggerty, Kevin and Ellerbrok, Ariane. *The Social Study of Serial Killers.* Crime and Justice. ND. Web.

Kari and Associates. *Delores "Dee" Davis.* Kari Sable Crime and Justice. June 26, 2006. Web.

Lady Blue. This is Why We Work. Mystic Snow Angel. February 26, 2005. Web.

Magnus, Eddie. *31 Years of the BTK Killer.* NBC News. August 12, 2005. Web

Murphy, Hannah, *BTK Serial Killer: What We Learned from Confessional Book.* Rolling Stone. September 12, 2016. Web.

Rossen, Rebecca J. *The Floppy Did Me In.* The Atlantic. January, 2014. Print.

Simpson, Stephanie and Huffstutter, P.J. *Clues Were Clear but Slow to Add Up.* LA Times. March 6, 2005.

Staff Writer. *Infamous BTK 'serial killer' reveals what drove him to torture and murder 10 people.* New Zealand Herald. September 3, 2018.Web

Staff Writer. *Victim's brother describes killing linked to BTK.* CNN. March 2, 2005. Web.

Wentzle, Roy. *Book Shows BTK as Selfish, Egoistical Bastard.* Wichita Eagle. August 18, 2016.

Wilgoren, Jodi. *In gory Detail the Prosecution Lays out Case for Tough Sentencing for BTK.* New York Times. August, 18, 2008. Print.